WAKE-UP CALL
וְכָפֶּשׁ־לָלַ

DR. JAMES W. GARNER
THE NAKED PROPHET

Copyright © 2024 **Dr. James Garner Publishing**

All rights reserved. No part of this publication may be reproduced, distributed, or transmitted in any form or by any means, including photocopying, recording, or other electronic or mechanical methods, without the prior written permission of the publisher, except in the case of brief quotations embodied in critical reviews and certain other noncommercial uses permitted by copyright law. For permission requests, write to the publisher, addressed "Attention: Book Rights and Permission," at the address below.

Published in the United States of America

ISBN 978-1-961507-32-6 (SC)
ISBN 979-8-89395-764-8 (Ebook)

Dr. James Garner Publishing
222 West 6th Street
Suite 400, San Pedro, CA, 90731
www.stellarliterary.com

Order Information and Rights Permission:

Quantity sales. Special discounts might be available on quantity purchases by corporations, associations, and others. For details, contact the publisher at the address above.

For Book Rights Adaptation and other Rights Permission. Call us at toll-free 1-888-945-8513 or send us an email at admin@stellarliterary.com.

CONTENTS

Look There at God's Design Plan 5
Revived Heart 6
I Have a Dream
Freedom for All 7
The Rainbow 8
Warrior's Statement of Faith in Yahovah 9
Nicene Creed 12
Apostles' Creed 13
Instead Of 14
The Son Is Rising 15
Time and Place 16
The Super Bowl Word 18
The New Dawn Word 23
The Earth Is Changed
The New Apostolic Age 30
In the Beginning Was the Spoken Word 36
I Am the New Samurai 38
Only by the Blood Of Yahshua 39
Walk With the Spirit of Yah!
Walk This Way with Me My Sons and Daughters! 41
A Call to All to Wake Up 43
Let My People Go 46
Reveal My Destiny!
It Has Been Revealed! 48
To Know the Word 50
I Am Nazir
I Am a Nazarite 51
To My Apostles in Training 52
You Are My Disciple 55
The Coming of the New Kingdom 58
I, Yashua, Will Walk into the Promise Land 61

The Law and the Spirit	62
I Am a Warrior!	
I Am a Warrior in the Army of my Yah!	63
Unless You Are Born Again	65
Psalm 119 The Hebrew Alphabet	66
Woe to Those Who Do Not Take Heed to My Word, the Spirit of Truth	134
You Will Come Falling Down	139
Virus/שרס	142
The Beginning of the New Day	
It Is Hereby Proclaimed	146
The Earth Will Transform into the Image of the Christ Yahshua	150
The Sword of Yahvah	152
Isiah 58	
How to Honor Yehovah in True Worship	154
The New Knight of the Realm	157
Declare	158
Prophesy	160
Who Is That Guy!	162
I Am a Living Tree	167
Twenty-Four Oxen All Together Yoked	169
It Is Hereby Proclaimed!	173
His Preliminary Speech	177
Let Us Do What We Were Born to Do!	179
The Lord Yahovah's Vengeance Will Be Their Pain Now!	180
On That Day, a Pleasant Vineyard Will Arise	
Sing About It	182
Psalm 17	184
The Twelve Commandments	186
Sons And Daughters of Yahvah	188
The Comparision of Human Beings and or Primates	190
At The Beginning Of The New Age	196
Dimentional Traveling	198
Don't Worry Be Happy	199
Holy Anointing Oil	200
I Will Change Your Name To Son Of The Living Yahovah!	201
I Am A Living Tree	202
I Am A Priest I Am A Priest I Am A Priest	205
Appendix	207
About The Author	209

LOOK THERE AT GOD'S DESIGN PLAN

Plants grows seed
Bird eats seed
Bird flies
Kraps seed out
Plant grows
Hypothesis
Plants have a job
Seeds have a job
Birds have a job
Kraps got a job

REVIVED HEART
רֹשֶׁךָ הֲרָת

Oh, Yahvah,
Open our eyes so we would see the way day or night,
Open our ears so that we could hear your words clearly,
Open our minds so we would understand your will completely,
Open our hearts so that we could feel compassion once again in every respect,
Open our nostrils so that we could smell the presence of your visitations always.

JWG 9/18/92

I HAVE A DREAM
FREEDOM FOR ALL

I

I say to you today, my friend, even though we face the difficulties of today and tomorrow. I still have a dream. It is a dream deeply rooted in the American dream.

I have a dream that one day this nation will rise up and live out the true meaning of its creed: "We hold these truths to be self-evident; that all men are created equal."

I have a dream that my four little children will one day live in a nation where they will not be judged by the color of their skin but by the content of their character.

I have a dream that one day every valley shall be exalted, every hill and mountain shall be made low, the rough places will be made plain . . . This is our hope . . . With this faith we will be able to transform the jangling discords of our nation into a beautiful symphony of the brotherhood.

And when this happens, and when we allow freedom to ring, when we let it ring from every village and every hamlet, from every state and every city, we will be able to speed up that day when all of God's children, black men and white men, Jews and Gentiles, Protestants and Catholic, will be able to join hands and sing in the words of that old Negro spiritual: "Free at last! Free at last! Thank God Almighty, we are free at last!"

-Martin Luther King Jr.

THE RAINBOW וּבֹנֶ־יר

ר־נִבוּ

אַר־נִבוּ תִהֶרַ וִלִל ־לִזִ־יִס בַ
אַ ־ סיאוּלא ללוֹ רֶהַת וּבֹנָאר אַ

A rainbow there will always be. There will always be a rainbow as a sign of my covenant with those who are my servants, who walk with me and give Yahovah their whole heart, not religion, I have hidden the rainbow in a rock, so there will always be a rainbow stored up somewhere. There will always be a rainbow as my eternal promise to you and to remind you that I have given you all things to use in moderation. The whole earth is to be subdued in moderation and temperance. And all of its resources are to be used for the betterment of all mankind. It is also my eternal promise to all of mankind of their inheritance in Christ Jesus and a glimpse of what the glory cloud around my throne looks like always.

    The double rainbow is a sign of my double-portion blessing that will come on America and on my children throughout the earth who have given me their whole heart forever. I will never flood the face of the whole earth ever again. I did not call you to practice religion. I called you to have a relationship with me, your only Yah. This is so that you will learn my ways and not the ways of the world.

JWG 10/16/11

WARRIOR'S STATEMENT OF FAITH IN YAHOVAH

We believe

#1 the Holy Spirit-filled Bible is the word of Yahshua, spoken to men and women of faith in Yah spiritually and audibly, and that there are many other Holy Spirit-filled books that have been written by spirit-filled believers of faith in Christ, which help all gain greater faith, insight, and discernment of the Holy Bible. Within itself is a collection of holy books. (Romans 1:16-17)

#2 there is one true great I Am (Yahvah) who has existed eternally in three personal identities: Father (Yahvah), Son, Jesus the Christ (Yahshua), and the Holy Spirit. (John 1:1-10; John 12:44-46)

#3 in the divinity of Christ, his virgin birth, his humble life as a man on earth, teaching all to love one another just as he unconditionally loves all, his healing power and miracle-filled life, his death on the cross for the sins of mankind, his return from the dead with the keys of hell, releasing the captives, his return to the earth to bear witness to the believers in Christ his ascension to power and glory in the Father, his return again as dispensator of the Holy Spirit and recommissioning of the apostles and believers in the Holy Spirit, his place as gatekeeper and judge of redemption over all mankind that no man should enter the kingdom without believing upon him as Savior, the son of yah, and the Messiah, and his return to rule over this earth to judge and reign over all mankind. (John 3:14-18; Ephesians 4:1-10; 1 Peter 3:18-22)

#4 in being born again in the Holy Spirit, in being baptized again in the Holy Spirit, in being baptized by the holy fire of the Holy Spirit. It is absolutely essential for the redemptive process and the salvation of all mankind. Only through the power of the Holy Spirit is the new man transformed into a new person able to abstain from the sins of this world and live a godly lifestyle. We as Christians are to encourage, exhort, and edify all believers, because there is no condemnation for those who are in Christ Jesus. (Ezekiel 36:26; John 13:13-20; James 3:13-18; 1 John 3:23-24)

#5 in miracles and the healing power of the Lord Jesus and that he heals and performs miracles today just as he did in the days of old through all Spirit-filled believers. All can pray and/or lay hands on the sick, but all may not have the specific gift of healing. He is not a distant Yah but an ever-present help. (Exodus 34:10; 1 Kings 17:22; Matthew 7:7-8)

#6 in that he gives to all the ability of grace, faith, visions, administration skills, helps words of knowledge, words of wisdom, prophetic words, discernments, distinguishing of spirits, various kinds of tongues, and the interpretation of tongues, just as he did yesterday. All are entitled to these giftings, but they may not be operating in them because of religiosity. (1 Corinthians 12:14; Mark 16:15-28; Daniel 2:20-23)

#7 in the true fivefold ministry. That is, there are apostles, prophets, evangelists, teachers, pastors, today just as it was in the days of old, just as our Lord stated in the Holy Bible. Until he comes again, all can minister even though they may not be chosen or gifted for one or more of these specific tasks or giftings. (Romans 1:1-6; 1 Corinthians 12:27-31; Ephesians 4:11-12)

#8 in the real unity of all Christian believers regardless of denominational faiths through the working of the Holy Spirit and the Lord Jesus Christ. The Lord's desire is for all Christian believers to walk in real unity of spirit and a true walk of love in real unconditional service of the Lord's cause. We will walk with A heart of peace and unity. (Psalm 133; Acts 4:32; Philippians 2:1-2; Ephesians 4:1-17)

#9 in walking by faith and not by sight. Faith is the assurance of things hoped for, the conviction of things not seen. By faith we understand that the worlds were prepared by the word of Yah so that what is seen was not made out of thing which are visible. (Hebrews 11)

#10 in worshiping the Lord Yahvahshua with all our heart, spirit, and strength. We understand that standing up, dancing, shouting, making a joyful noise, lifting up of hands, and the playing of music with guitars, drums, harps, cymbals, etc., are fundamental part of worshipping from the heart and spirit. The Davidic spirit demands this type of worship. (Deuteronomy 6:5; Psalm)

#11 in that the great commission to all Spirit-filled believers is to go out into the entire earth and preach the Gospel to all flesh using every means possible to do so. To save souls for the kingdom of Yahshua. (Mark 16:15-18; Luke 14:16-24)

#12 in that there is a heaven and a hell, a resurrection of the saved and the lost, the saved who have accepted the Lord Yahshua as son of Yah and gatekeeper and those souls who have not learned to love, who have remained bitter and unforgiving, who have not attained this great unconditional love. (John 15:1-11)

#13 in that we must daily pray, repent, and dedicate ourselves to the Lord continually, having an open heart to hear the Lord's voice and direction for our daily life, always willing to do the work of the Lord Yahshua, respecting his authority over our daily life. (Ephesians 6)

Written in the spirit by James W. Garner

NICENE CREED

We believe in one Yah, Yahovah the Elohim, the all powerful, maker of the heavens and earth, of all that is seen and unseen.

We believe in one Yashua Yahmashic, the only living son of Yahovah, eternally begotten of the Elohim, Yah from Yah, light from light, true Yah from true Yah, begotten not made, being one in substance with Yahovah. Through him all things were made. For us men and our salvation came down from heaven, by the power of the Holy Spirit, he was born of the Virgin Mary, and became a man.

For our sake he was crucified under Pontious Pilate; he suffered died, and was entombed. He descended unto the dead and set the captives free.

On the third day he rose again from the dead in fulfillment of the scriptures; he ascended into heaven and is seated at the right hand of the Elohim. He will come again in glory to judge the living and the dead, and his kingdom will have no end.

We believe in the Holy Spirit, the Lord and giver of life, who proceeds from the Elohim and the Son. With the Elohim and the Son he is worshipped and glorified. He was spoken of through the prophets.

We believe in the unity of the church. We acknowledge one baptism for the remission of sins. We look for the resurrection of the dead, and the life of the renewed world to come at the return of Yahshua, Amen.

APOSTLES' CREED

I believe in one Yahovah, the only Elohim Almighty, creator of all the heavens, the earth, our universe, and all the galaxies.

I believe in Yahshua, the only Christ, Yahovah's only begotten son, our savior and a redeemer.

Yahshua was named and conceived by the Holy Spirit, born of the Virgin Mary.

Yahshua was tortured under Pontious Pilate, was crucified on the cross, died the same day, and was buried the same day.

Yahshua descended into the gates of hell, took the keys from his brother Lucifer and set the captives free.

On the third day Yahshua rose from the dead and ascended into heaven, and is seated at the right hand of the Father.

Yahshua will come again to judge the living and the dead.

I believe in the Holy Spirit, the unity of churches, the communion of saints, the forgiveness of all sins, the resurrection of the spirit and body, and life everlasting without end. Amen. Selah.

INSTEAD OF

Instead of the fortunes I had planned for you, you have set your eyes on bobbles and beads, cursing instead of blessing, gossiping instead of speaking the truth. You must take heed or that shall be what I will give you.

You must take heed to my words and the words of my true minister and prophets that don't speak the way you want. That don't look the way you want. That don't walk the way you want. That don't dance the way you want.

They are the way I want them to be, says Yahovah, the Elohim.

James Garner 8/31/09

THE SON IS RISING

The Son is risen and is raised to his place in heaven. Now is the Son's time to rise again. The dawn of the new day has already begun, and the past is in the distance of obscurity. Now is the time for a chance. It is the time for a chance, but the time will come for no chances left at all. The time for me to come again will come. Do not take a chance that it will not happen. I am your only Yah. I am the Lord of Lords and the light of all lights, the only Yah of all the heavens, Yahvahshua.

Stay close to me or you will just die.
Walk close to me. Never retreat.
Keep your eyes on me every day.
A time for a chance.
A time for no chances left at all.
A time for me to come.
A time for me to come again.

James Garner 9/31/09

TIME AND PLACE

There is a time and place for everything under the son of Yah!
There is a time to come to the earth and a time to leave this earth.
A time to rise up again and a time to come back again.
To be born then be born again.
To plant and sow seed and then reap your harvest.
A time to hold back your seed and not give it to the swine.
A time to let them go and a time to hold them back.
A time to turn the page in the positive direction and a time to stop and think.
A time to be born and a time to die.
A time to be killed and a time to die respectfully.
A time for joy and a time to mourn.
A time to heal it and a time to kill it.
A time to tear down and a time to build it up.
A time to build it now and a time to leave it vacant.
A time to cry and a time to laugh.
A time to boogie and a time to dance.
A time to march right through and a time to stroll right in.
A time to walk and a time to run.
A time to cast things away and a time gather things up.
A time to embrace and a time to refrain from embracing.
A time to win and a time to lose.
A time to pick up and a time to put down.
A time to keep it and time to throw it away.
A time to rend and a time to sew.
A time to be silent and a time to speak loudly.
A time to jab and a time to throw a left hook.
A time to duck and a time to step back.
A time to bob and a time to weave.
A time to restore it and a time to send it to the scrap yard.

WAKE UP CALL

A time to love and a time to hate.

A time for beauty and a time for ashes.
A time for war and a time for peace.
A time to delegate according to seniority and a time to give the job to the right person.
A time for a chance and a time for no chances left at all.
A time to respect and a time to disrespect.
A time to listen to losers and so lose.
A time for me to come and a time for me to come back again.

It's time to wake up, climb out of the spiderweb, and get your eyes right on Yahovah, because your time for a chance is coming to an end. Then there will be no chances left at all.

JWG/His Way Ministries 12/12/10

THE SUPER BOWL WORD

02/03/02

Dear Fellow Servant of the Lord Jesus,

My name is James William Garner.

As the year started, I was told by the Lord that I am released. I was not fully released into the ministry until now, although the Lord has allowed me to dance and minister in the background, or MIB, from my childhood to the present.

The Lord also told me to watch what he was going to do in the NFL playoffs and the Super Bowl this year, that it would be a prophetic miracle and that he could move in any kingdom of a man as he a chooses to show that he is in control. To show that the kingdoms of this world are not to be thrown away like many false, misleading leaders say, but overtaken by the kingdom of our Lord Yahshua. As the Lord says, "The kingdoms of this world will become the kingdoms of our Lord Yahshua" and also "to proclaim it on the mountaintops."

On Super Bowl Sunday, the Lord put a lot of people looking at one thing on one day in one place in America. He has the largest worldwide live audience in the world. People of all types and all backgrounds watched the game on Sunday. The Lord somehow put all these different people and got them to sing about freedom and unity around the whole live television world. This also was the largest-ever gathering of different nations to watch a ballgame, and more people than ever in the history of the world sang about freedom, peace, and unity. This must be something that's' on the Lord's heart.

WAKE UP CALL

My favorite team is the Rams, but somehow I thought that the Patriots would pull off an upset the same as with the Steelers and the Raiders. Well, sometimes your judgement gets clouded by favoritism.

As the playoffs started, two teams emerged as the winners: one from the American Football Conference (the Patriots) and one from the National Football Conference (The Rams). The Patriot was the team that was overlooked and thought to be the losers. They then became the champions. They beat the best team in the NFL, and the key to the whole thing and the only reason they won was the team's unity of spirit and courage.

As the game started, the first song was played by Paul by McCartney, the father of the rock 'n' roll revolution, and Wings. The first song on the Lord's heart was "Talking about Freedom."

Freedom of spirits is one of the keys to this unshakable unity. The Lord wants freedom within his churches and this and this country formed in the name of Yah. The Lord wants prophets with vision back in the church culture. They are the eyes of the church. Without them, there is no vision. The Lord is tired dictators. He wants teams, clans, or tribes in unity, to fulfill the same goal-that is, saving souls. We now have a limited time to sow for the greatest harvest of souls that will ever be. There is still a chance for unity before judgement. In one moment in time, the Lord got the peoples of the world to proclaim freedom throughout the world. The Lord got the peoples of the world proclaimed unity as well.

As the teams came out to play, the Lord was talking about unity and that if the church will not unify on its own and that since no pastor is or will step up to the plate, he will have to start a new thing with a new breed of man that will listen to his heart and not their own. And that on a team where unity is in disarray, it would be impossible to win any war this way because of disunity. The day of the one-man show is over.

Then as the national anthem was played, it seemed to have new deeper meaning to it. Over our history, we have always rallied behind the flag, which stands for the trinity of unity.

The second set of songs on the Lord's heart came together. The first song U2 played was the song "Beautiful Day." It's a brand-new day, and you too can play in this new day. Everything done from old religious formulas of the past will no longer work. It is the starting of the new day for mankind. You too can play in a brand-new day-the days where we speak to the Jordan and/or speak to the altar of rocks so that the mountains can be removed and the angels can be released from the mountaintops and the country of angels. It is simple. We as men make it religious and too deep in the doctrines of men, a box the Lord will not live in. Yah is too big for this box we all make for him. Yah will show the way.

The second song was "Where the Streets Have No Name." The Lord is going to do this thing in a place where the streets have no name. The Lord is tired of the wounded warriors being discarded and treated as trash because of the way the Lord has made them look. The Lord is going to pick up those warriors that have been discarded by the religious church system. The overlooked, the discarded, the wounded, and the left behind-these are the ones that will make a change in this world. "They will arise as my true champions. Yes, they will arise," says the Lord "These are the ones who have truly given me their heart and want to be my true friend, whom I can come to trust and rest in true love."

The favored team almost won the game. They almost went into overtime but was lost at the last minute because of confusion in the defense-confusion and disunity.

The favored team was supposed to win the game, but they did not and cannot till or unless they unite or be judged. The favored team is The Lord's churches united as one unit with one goal. They are failing because of old pet peeves that really make no difference other than the fact that they wish to be religious and worship their old dead idols instead of having a relationship with the Lord. Because there is no fear of the Lord in the church, there is no understanding. Because Proverbs say, "The fear of the Lord is the beginning of understanding."

"It's time to release my champion underdogs. To do what nobody thought could be done," says the Lord of Hosts. "They are patriots, and they deeply love my country."

Final score was Rams 17, Patriots 20.

A patriot is loyal, loving, trustworthy, united, and zealous. He believes in life, liberty, freedom, unity, and the pursuit of good things, for the betterment of the whole team. A team such as this would be unstoppable.

WAKE UP CALL

This is the Lord's country. It was founded upon his name by men with sheer courage who believed in the Lord wholeheartedly. Our forefathers worked as a team to build a new nation established under Yah. When our forefathers sat down to write the Constitution and the Bill of Rights, the Lord was with them. This government is his government, formed by the Lord himself.

The judicial system is the Lord's. The Lord Yahshua holds the balance in his right hand. He is the true and righteous judge. He hears the cries of the people being railroaded through the system in the name of justice. He hears the cries of those who have committed no crime and are innocent, framed by the system. The lord wants true justice and true peace.

The school system is the Lord's school system. Just because the churches decided to abandon them and stop praying for them does not mean that they're still not the Lord's. The Lord hears the cries of the grandmothers, mothers, and children. He hear the cries for justice and true peace.

The Lord wants radical sweeping changes to be made. If we all don't step up to the plate, the Lord will be forced to bring judgement himself. The Lord wants you to be a patriot.

These are the scriptures the Lord gave me after the game:

> When David was released to fight Goliath, in 1 Samuel 17:20, "So David arose early in the morning and left the flock with a keeper and took the supplies and went as his father Jesse had commanded him. And he came to the circle of the camp while the army was going out in battle array shouting the war cry."
>
> If we listen to the Lord, we will be supplied as we step out by faith. As we step out by faith and combat our true adversary, the devil and his minions, we will win with the first stone we speak to.

2 Samuel 17:20, "You will cross the Jordan."

Psalm 17, prayer for protection from oppressors.

Psalm 20, prayer for victory over enemies.

Matthew 17:20, "Because of the littleness of your faith; for truly I say to you, if you have faith as mustard seed, you shall say to this mountain, 'Move from here to there,' and it shall move; and nothing shall be impossible to you."

John 17:20, "I don't ask in behalf of these alone, but for those also who believe in me through their word; that they may all be one even as thou, father, art in me, and I in thee, that they also will be in us; that the world may believe that thou did send me."

Revelation 17.

I am writing you today to let you know that I will step up to the plate. I am an apostolic Nazarite prophet of the Lord Yahshua. I am the burning man from the desert, a flaming torch for Yahshua. The Lord has commanded me to form a team to change the world, to make changes in LA County, California, and then the nation and the world. We have some major obstacle to overcome, some major principalities and powers to contend with. This takes unity of spirits and freedom. Once we all band together, we will have superior covering of protection. I hope that we can talk about this further. Let us look with eyes of faith and see what the Lord will do through us. I pray the Lord would touch your heart to move on this endeavor. We have full semitruck loads of seeds to dump. We have time still to do it. Let's get to it.

The Lord bless you and your house.

James W. Garner
Prophet of our Lord Yahshua

THE NEW DAWN WORD

Dear fellow servant of the Lord Jesus Christ,

I proclaim this, this day of May 19, 2002. It is now the new dawn of the new age of the twenty-first century. This has become the age of the great spiritual awakening and revolution for mankind. A new age of investment in the youth of the world has begun, to show them the real Jesus, the Lord of love, to wake up the youth and show them the real Jesus.

A new age for mankind's renewal has begun! A chance to make a change for good in the new millennium. A change in your church doctrine and all you've invested in it. Investment in your investment on good ground to bring unity to the body of Christ. Also a chance in your community and your investment there, your country and your investment there.

A new age of judgements has begun! An age of judgements between what has been done right and wrong and what will be the done to correct it. The engine seems to need an overhaul. All those ministries that continue to make money off the Lord Jesus and do not operate by his ways will have a spiritual and natural death. Those who are not supposed to be in the ministry will be removed by the Lord. Those who use the Lord for their own greedy ambitions and gain will be removed and not be able to operate.

Jesus the Christ must be lifted up and not men.

A new age of taking action has begun! An age of taking action to cause a better outcome. It's not the time to be acting the same as it ever was. It's simple, but we as men make it complicated.

A new age of curse breaking has begun! A new age of all the curses being broken off mankind. Because of this new dawn for mankind, the two-thousand-year curse has been broken to pieces by Yahvahshua and his angelic armies.

As a result of this change, all things have been changed in the spirit realm. As a result of this change, there are new releases of holy angels, new releases of new special apostolic gifting, new releases of apostolic order, new releases in mighty miracles of healing, new releases in miraculous healing, new releases of visions and dreams, new releases in miraculous signs and wonders, new releases in fivefold ministry gifting, a new release of apostolic order to cleanse the temple and establish order for the house of the Lord Jesus-to establish the government of the Lord for the house of the Lord Jehovah. These apostolic knights will accomplish all the assignments of the Lord Yahvahshua, and their rakes will never be broken by man or spirit.

This letter being sent out as a wake-up call for all those who are in any ministry or those who wish to move into their own new ministry. The new millennial season of seven years of spiritual planting has now started, with two years of church leadership as a whole doing much of nothing and treating things as if business was as usual, or they were off on their calculations. We still have five years left for the religious church system to wake up and go by what the ways of Yah say to do and not the religious churches traditions of men. Your religious image won't matter in hell.

During this period of time, it would be good to be looking at foundations, if they are correct. Who do you think has laid your foundation, a man or Yahshua? Has it been prepared properly by the Holy Spirit and not a man? Is there a better way to do this Jesus thing? Get born again. Get baptized by the blood of fire. Jesus said, "You can't see if you're not baptized by fire from the Holy Spirit" to get freed from the chains that bound us by religion the very thing Jesus fought the most.

Look at the soil to see if the dirt is ready for the spiritual seed to be planted and not wasted. Test-plant to see what's been put in the spiritual dirt by the enemy. Then thoroughly take out all the spiritual diseases, bugs, and parasites so that we can grow a truthful and honest victory church, with knights whose armor never fades because they found the truth and it set them free of the chains that bound them.

These are things that exist in the spirit and must be fought in the spirit. This new war is a spiritual war. If you don't accept, it doesn't matter; it will happen anyway. If you do nothing, it will get worse. If you wait for Jesus to come, he'll laugh at you and say your works mean nothing to him and throw you in the fire. You were called to do something. You were saved to make a difference. You were saved to make a change in history. That's why you have a free will to choose which pathway to follow. Wake up and see the light. You can speak it into existence. You can make it happen. You can do it. If you can hear, hear the word given to the new church of the living God. Open your ears to hear.

You can make a choice.
You can make a change
You can make a new foundation.
You can make a unity as one and yet be diverse.
You can make a difference.
You can make a free but different choice.
You can make a better future.

We are now at a judgment time for the religious church and all of mankind. Are you going to continue to put your thumb in the Lord Jehovah's face? The fear of the Lord is the beginning of understanding. Mankind now holds its own fate in its own hands- either to follow the pathway of renewal and peace or devastation and self-destruction. If the religious Christian church continues to operate by the tradition of men and not the traditions of Yah, their ministries will die in the transition, just as Moses and most of the original Israelites died in the desert and did not enter into the Promised Land. They didn't cross the Jordan because they wanted the old things they had in Egypt. They would not change with the times. They wanted the past and not the future. They were not happy with angel's foods and no sickness. They wanted religion, not relationship. Only those who could see the promise in the future entered into the promise. Joshua and Caleb were tested in the desert for forty years before they entered into the promise given them. Ever since the beginning, they live for the promise that was given them, looking into the future for the promise given.

They took it by faith to go on the offensive and take action to receive the promise given them and the country. By taking action, they stepped out in faith and received the promise given them. They refused to live under the curse any longer and received the promise. They looked into the future and received the promise. All had to take action together to get to the Promise Land. Every tribe had to help seize the Promise Land. Everyone had to take part. Everyone had to speak it into existence.

We are now at war in America in the natural. But there have been wars and rumors of wars since the death of Jesus. Also in the spirit realm, a war has been going on since the fall of Satan from heaven. But most people seem to want to be blind to it in the natural, even though the Bible says to trust in what you can't see and not in what you can see. A new war has broken out in the spirit and is going on in the spirit. It is a covert war, and the enemy has spun a web of illusions, deceit, and mistrust in the Lord. So instead we should be sowing seeds of the truth, justice, peace, discipline, and self control. But webs burn in the fire just like everything else will in the end. So it's time to shout to the peoples of the earth, "Wake up! The great and terrible day of the Lord is at hand and has been at hand for two thousand years." Get it! Since the day John The Baptist proclaimed it.

The two-thousand-year curse has been broken and removed by the Lord Yahvahshua. So now is the time at hand to

get tough,
get real,
get focused on Jesus,
get alive in Christ,
be born again in the true Holy Spirit,
get filled with the new wine of the living Christ,
get whole again with the great I Am,
get the blood of Jesus pumping through your veins.

Now is the time to stare at the stars in heaven and wonder at God's glory and majesty, not to see all the stars we have and blunder.

"It is the ultimate wonder to see the son of thunder in all his wonder come down and visit us asunder."

Jesus is the ultimate act of submission. He has been exalted before all men. Yahshua came teaching that salvation was centered in a person and has to do with attitudes and with personal relationships of acceptance, forgiveness, love, and faith. This message of love goes contrary to established traditions of the church systems.

We now have millions of American youth who have never been taught discipline, who have never had any kind of father, let alone a spiritual one. These youth are searching for something good in a place that seems godless. Lots of teenagers are finding it in drugs, a false sense of love, not real love, They also see through the old traditions of the past. They have to be shown something real-a real relationship with our Father and creator, the great I Am. They need to be shown the power of the infinite living God in the real way. They want to be born again with the real Holy Spirit. They need to be taught a disciplined lifestyle free from religious persecution. They don't need to be brainwashed with scripture. They need to be given a Holy Spirit-filled Bible that shows them the real Jesus and not religion. They need spiritual meat, not a baby bottle. Yahshua's gospel of love goes contrary to established traditions.

The number 1 rule of war is to know your enemy. Most Christians do not know the enemy because the enemy is in the spirit. They do not even acknowledge the existence of the spirit realm or Satan. The religious spirit is the unholy ghost. Satan works in reverse. It always has, and that is one of its limitations. It also reverts to fear tactics. Control tactics are the fruit of Satan and are in every church in one traditional form or another, the traditions of men and not the Lord Yahshua's. The religious laws and traditions kill the joy of the Holy Spirit. The Holy Spirit brings new life to the earth. The Holy Spirit serves new life and the Lord Yah. The devil wants you to walk by sight and not by faith.

So what can we do? Be more aware. If you asked and prayed for discernment, open your eyes so you can see it. It is time to wake up from the spiderweb. The unholy trinity must not be allowed to operate anywhere, especially a church of the Lord Jesus Christ. Jezebel, Ahab, and the unholy ghost are satanic spirits of religion. Of course, Satan would want to set up himself in the false god position. He's given himself many names over the centuries and gotten men to worship his false religions.

Another rule of war is, divide and conquer. This tactic seems to be its favorite. This was how he started infiltrating the Christian church systems. We must want to develop an intrepid spirit of fearfulness and teamwork. This act of real unity and teamwork is something Satan has no way to stop. This is what will defeat him and his own lies. This is why he fights so hard against unity. The only real power Satan has is to deceive. By default on the part of many Christians, Satan has power over their lives by receiving the unholy ghost or the curse laid on them. He also knows he is a loser. He has lost every battle beforehand. He's already been totally defeated. He is the father of all lies. He has already lost every battle before they even started. Wake up, kick him out of your life forever. Evil will be beaten by love. Don't tolerate him in your life any longer. Satan's rule over you is dependent on people knowingly or unknowingly allowing him to rule over their lives.

You can believe the truth or suffer the consequences. All prophecy is given to make a change. The choice to make a difference is yours. Why not make a difference? The gospel of the kingdom comes through God in us.

The Lord gave this scripture, Zechariah 8:11-17:

> "But now I will not treat the remnant of this people as in the former days," declares the Lord of hosts. "For I declare there will be peace for the seed: all the trees and vines will yield its fruit, the land will yield its produce, and the heavens will give their dew; and I will cause the remnant of these people to inherit the earth. And it will come about that just as you were a curse among the nations, oh house of Jesus and house of Israel, so I will save you that you may become blessing. Do not fear! Let your hands be strong." For thus says the Lord of hosts, "And I have not relented, so I again in these days propose to do a good thing to all mankind. Do not fear! These are things you all should do: speak the truth to one another; judge with truthful judgement as if it were you for peace within your houses. Also let none of you devise evil in your heart against one another, and do not love perjury; for all these are what I hate," says the lord of hosts.

WAKE UP CALL

To him that has ears to hear, let him fear the word given to the religious church system.

Let the love of God encompass you.
Let the truth set you free.
Let the peace that passes all understanding cover you.
Let the atonement for sin lead you.
The Lord said, "Speak to the rock and it will bring forth a river of life."
If you'd like to talk further.
The Lord bless you and your house,

James W. Garner
Apostolic prophet of our Lord Yahvahshua

THE EARTH IS CHANGED THE NEW APOSTOLIC AGE

06/06/04

It is hereby proclaimed the world is changed. It is a new day! A different time and season for the purpose of change in heaven and earth. To everything given, there is a time and a season. Therefore, for every season, there is a time. There has been a season for every time and a time for every age, because the earth is in perpetual motion into the future and is always set in a state of change, growth, and renewal from old to new.

In this way, nature is set up to change from old to new annually according to time and season.

For the Lord, Yahovah, has set change on the breath of tomorrow's future and the rise and fall of the new day's breeze. As things are set up in a natural way by Yahshua, so are they in the spirit world with one big exception to it.

The spirit and soul are set to transcend time, never knowing by sight where the future lies. Only by faith does man transcend time, never knowing by sight where the future lies. Only by faith does man transcend time and step into the future. The old age has ended; the new dawn age has begun!

Can you not see the earth is different somehow? The dawn and the sunset have somehow been changed by the hand of Yah!

The Lord, Yahovah, in heaven, changes times and seasons to suit his purpose under the Son, not ours. A season of time has passed away, and a new season has begun! The former things have passed away, and it's time for a new awakening for the earth and mankind. The season of time has come for all things to be revealed by the hand of Yah. We need drastic change of the right kind. If the old order won't step up to the plate, Yahshua will stand up to the plate with his newly trained disciples!

So where idols once stood, Yahshua will stand, with fire in his eyes!

Are you going to religiously stand against Yahshua because he's saving people you don't want saved? Or as a friend? Or has he stopped blessing you because all you do when you come into his presence is ask for things, instead of worshipping the Lord Yahovah and believing he's already given it into your hands? All things come to pass in their own time, at the season and time destined for their change. As a result, if you continue to do things according to the old ways or by the traditions of men or religiously, they will not work as they worked in past dispensations.

Without changing with time, those people who will continue to try to hold on to the powers of the past will fall by them. History is repeating itself far too often. It's time to walk away from the past and step into the future.

Tomorrow is a better day than yesterday. Because the hand of Yahshua in the spirit realm has changed all things, the old age has passed, and a new century has come to hand. The age is over, and times have changed for the better. It is now time for Yahshua's one-thousand-year reign to install his new order. Those who try to rule the world by their greedy ambitions for money and power will be tortured by it. The acceptable time of the Lord's reign is at hand. It is now also the time to take Hasatan, his minions, and his unholy trinities in a thousand years of chains and pains.

"I can see it upon the winds of the heavens. Open the eyes of my heart to see the great change and act upon it. I can hear it roaring across the still waves. Open the ears of my heart to hear Yahshua's words and act upon them. I can smell it in the fires of the deep, burning. Open the nose of my heart to smell out the way cautiously forward. I can fully perceive it standing on the mountaintops of the earth. Open the senses of my heart to perceive all obstacles and over-take them with discipline. I can feel it touching my senses in the spirit realm. Open the deep of my heart. Touch it deeply to feel your holy presence always."

The earth has changed, the season and time has come at hand, and the fires of change have been lit and are trimmed and burning. I smell it flowing across the winds of the air. They new day's streams are running freely, and the old well has gone dry and will produce no more sweet waters. The old guard is still trying to hold on to the past dispensations, when a new day has begun. A new spring has sprung up, and it has sweet water running from it. Its living waters can never be dammed up, and they flow freely throughout the earth.

All the principalities and powers hear the warning gong sounding. Their time is up; they have to give it all up, for it all was temporarily theirs.

All I have to do is walk into the enemy's stronghold and take back all he has stolen from me. All things are Yah's, and by his hands he institutes and disposes. All the angels are rejoicing; the new day has come. The time of the release of all the captives is at hand, and those held in the graves of the deep, wishing for redemption, have and will be redeemed by the blood and body of the Lamb of God.

Thus, says the Lord of Hosts, "If you say you can no longer hear my voice, or feel my touch, or see my face maybe we have somehow broken our friendship and fellowship by your following the teachings of men and not that of the living Yah or his teachings or ways."

Yahshua (Jesus) needs disciples, not followers. If I don't have the love, friendship, or power of Yah, then you have nothing at all. All you children of the Lord Yahovah are being called to grow up and become disciples and not followers. Otherwise, you're just another lamb being led to the slaughterhouse.

"The winds of change are blowing. The rivers of change are flowing; the earth is quaking at this great shaking. For all the spirits, there is a knowing. The horns of change are going to be blowing. The fires of change are raising smoke and burning."

The Holy Spirit is leading this new-dawn teaching.

I can feel it standing upon the roll of the running wave. I can smell it in the flowing air. I can see it in the shining stars above. I can hear its presence upon the quiet earth. I can feel his holy touch inside of me, and it quickens the deep of my spirit and gives me confidence to walk in truth, love, and peace always.

I can walk into the dawn of true deep peace.
I see it upon the earth. Change.

WAKE UP CALL

I feel its touch upon the waters. Change.
I hear it in the air waves. Change.
I smell it in the fires of incense before the Lord. Change.
I feel it in the spirit realm. Change.
The earth has been changed.

"All you children of the Lord are being called to grow up and come into his presence with worship, not complaints. If I don't have the blessing of Yah, then I have nothing at all. Oh, my people, can't you hear me calling your names?"

The eyes of my heart are open to this natural and spiritual change. I can only imagine how great a change you have made in the spirit realm. If I can see it upon the face of the deep, how great a change have you made, of mighty Yah of my fathers?

Heaven and earth are now set to behold your glory. For it is the will of all creation and the ambition of all matter to take part in this new day creation, oh Yah of my fathers. I perceive it in the consciousness of my mind's eyes, and the earth quakes at the change.

I see it being revealed thoroughly in the spirit world, and I see the fear and trembling cast upon the demonic realm. I feel its touch blowing upon the paths of the four winds, because their directions have been changed.

The directions of the tides have been changed; they now flow in new tidal patterns. The tides of all the battles have now turned in the disciple's favor!

I hear it in the sounds of the crashing of the waves upon the sands of time.

Things have changed for the better, not the worst!

I smell it in the smoke of the fires explosively burning throughout the earth's forests, and the aroma of that change could be smelled throughout the scorched earth.

All my senses have been opened up to this change, and I rejoice at it.
The weather patterns have changed, and new ones have begun!
The four winds have been turned and are blowing in new directions!
The rains will flow heavy and sweet throughout the earth again because the four winds have been turned in new directions!

The four directions have been sent out to tell the four winds to blow sweet and softly upon this world again!

The tides have now turned and are flowing in a new direction to bless the earth and not curse it anymore!

I breathe deeply and can smell it upon the mists of the rains flowing from the deep of the earth!

All false religion will come falling down with a mighty crash because of this new direction!

The weather patterns are my friends and must obey my commands!

The atmospheric conditions must bow their knees to me!

The gravitational forces of nature must obey my command and attract all mankind to the center Yahshua, the only Christ Messiah!

All particles of matter must obey my commands and arise!

There is no greater power than that given you and your generation, to make changes in the near future before the reign of Yahshua, the Christ Messiah!

The lightning and thunder roars at this new change in direction. The four winds set in new directions are howling change. The winds and clouds shake the earth with whirlwinds of change. The torrid flames of change are dancing on the winds of eternity's new directions. A bright, shiny day comes after the thunder and the rain. Pain comes before the rain; after the pain comes the gain.

You are the air I breathe!
I go nowhere without you!
You are my atmosphere!
I feel your presence inside of me in everything I do!
I go nowhere without you!
I breathe you out! I breathe you in!
Your Holy Spirit's breath is within my lungs, and it guides me!
Tender is your touch, and everlasting is your mercy!
The truth is spoken upon your voice, and it is everlasting!
I feel your presence inside me!
I can feel this new day change inside of me!
I can see this change all around me!
I can hear the winds of revolution turning!

WAKE UP CALL

I can taste the new flavor of change in the new future, and it's sweet!
I can smell something new is up-it's change!
I can speak into existence this great change!
I can see this change all around me now, and it gives me new strengths to act upon it!
Now is the right time for the right kind of change!
Now is the time to let Yah arise!
"Love opens the doors to renewal and change!
Be my eyes!
See my vision!
Be my ears!
Hear my vision!
Be my taste!
Perceive my vision!
Son of mine, be a revolution!
Get ready for major change in the future!"

IN THE BEGINNING WAS THE SPOKEN WORD
דרו׳ נכפּס הֶת סאו ננננבַ הֶת ת׳

At the beginning was the spoken word, and the word was spoken by Yah and was Yah! The spoken word was in the beginning with Yahvahshua only!

All things were spoken into existence by Yahvahsua, and without him, you have nothing at all!

Within him is the life force of nature, and that life force is that which ignited the light inside of mankind!

The lights shined on the darkness, and the darkness had to run from the light because they could not understand the kingdom of Yah and tried to become greater than the true light!

So Yahovah sent yet another man to testify to that light whose name was James (make change). He came to make change and to bear witness of the light of Yah. The true light wants change in the attitude of his people. Repentance.

Through him you would see the truth and be set free of the religious chains that bind you, to believe in the power within you, and the messiah is with him and his disciples and plans his return in this season of time.

He is not the light but was born and sent to bear witness and testify of that true light that lights all the earth and every human being that comes into this world and the next.

He lived in this time in this world, and the earth was formed and made by him, and the religious world chose to know him not.

He came to receive his own and to fulfill the word of Yah, but the religious were blinded by the light and could not see it because of the works of religion and the Antichrist.

But many opened their eyes and received him as a brother; to them he gave the power and dominion over the earth to become a son of Yah and a disciple of the living Yah, who are born of the blood and flesh of the living Christ and not the will of man but of Christ, and the word was made spirit and dwelt inside of those who would receive, and we beheld the glory of him by the indwelling of his Holy Spirit, full of grace, truth, and true inner peace.

James bears witness of this change in direction, and in the course of humanity, I have and will send more after me who have and will do greater works than I. And from the fullness of his bounty, we have received strength and power and grace for grace.

For the law was given by Yah to Moses and the prophets and was distorted by religious people of faith, but grace and truth come by Yah, Yahshua, and the Holy Spirit.

No man can see Yah in the flesh and still live. The patriarchs, the prophets, Yahshua, the disciples, and the apostles have declared his sovereignty and this is the record of James, who was sent to bring change in the attitude of the religious denominations who do not operate in Yah's ways.

I AM THE NEW SAMURAI

A disciplined, intrepid warrior who fears not death, he carries the shield of faith, which signifies his identity with Christ as his defense. He has the sword of the Spirit, which is the spoken word of Yah. He holds the torch of redemption whose light will shine on all darkness. He wears the helmet of salvation and the breastplate of righteousness that stops all assaults against the body, soul, and spirit. His breeches are held up with the buckle of charity and the belt of the gospel of truth. When spoken, it always, makes the enemy flee before them. He stands in boots humbly prepared to make peace or war in the dirt or on the floor. He has the body and blood of Yahshua inside him.

Being filled with the Holy Spirit and having the power of his might, they live for but one purpose: to further the gospel of Yahshua.

Peace, truth, love, redemption, and faith are the spoken word of our gospel, but we exist to fight all evil.

By the Holy Spirit
Judah Jedi Knights
JWG AEP

ONLY BY THE BLOOD OF YAHSHUA

It is hereby proclaimed!
Only by the blood and body and
Through the blood and body of Yahshua,
I am redeemed from the hands of the enemy!
Through the blood and body of Yahshua,
I am forgiven of all my sins, past and present!
Through the blood and body of Yahshua,
I am continually cleansed from all my sins!
Through the blood and body of Yahshua,
I am justified through Christ and made
Righteous as if I had never sinned!
Through the blood and body of Yahshua,
I am sanctified, made holy, and set apart in Yah!
Through the blood and body of Yahshua,
I am bold and can enter into the presence
Yahvahshua!
Through the blood and body of Yahshua,
I am covered by the blood of Yahshua, and it
Cries out continually to Yah on my behalf!
Through the blood and body of Yahshua,
I am more than a conqueror-I am an overcomer!
Through the blood and body of Yahshua,
I am a warrior for the Christ!
Through the blood and body of Yahshua,
I am a disciple of the living Christ, and he is my friend!
Through the blood and body of Yahshua,

JAMES GARNER

I have dominion over all things!
Through the blood and body of Yahshua,
I have been granted eternal life!
Through the blood and body of Yahshua,
My strength is continually renewed.
I will dance and not grow weary.

JWG 11/29/10

WALK WITH THE SPIRIT OF YAH! WALK THIS WAY WITH ME MY SONS AND DAUGHTERS!

(10/10/10)

I walk the way Yahovah walks in and by the power of Yahovah!

I perceive the Holy Spirit of Yahovah has touched me and given me the fruit of the Holy Spirit!

I have been touched by the Holy Spirit of Yahovah.

I have feet that walk the way he walks in the spirit, so now I walk the way Yahshua walks always.

I have hands that are made for battle that war in the spirit and the natural his way.

I have a mouth that speaks exactly what he speaks in the spirit and in truth.

I talk the way Yahshua talks through the spirit of the spoken word by the Holy Spirit.

I have the power to command it to be by the power of the spoken word of the Holy Spirit.

I have eyes that see clearly what Yahovah sees in the spirit, and he sees through my eyes.

I see what he sees.

I have ears that hear what the words of Yahovah are in the natural and in the spirit.

I hear the voice of Yahovah.

I have a nose that smells what Yahovah smells in the spirit and the real world.

I smell the fruit of the Holy Spirit.

I have a mind that thinks the way Yahovah thinks and believes in the spirit of the spoken word spoken in the spirit of Yahovah.

I have dreams and visions that show me the pathway to take every day.

I have a heart that loves the way Yahovah unconditionally forever loves all who give their hearts to him and walk in the spirit with him.

I love you, oh Yahovah, my strength.

Yahovah has given me all the tools to complete the job given to me when he chose me in the womb. I must learn to use them all properly and in the spirit with him at my side, covering me in his blood and eternal glory. The older I become, the more strength and vitality I will have because I walk the way he walked. I will grow stronger, not weaker, every day because tomorrow will be a new day. Yahovah's hands are always full of our daily supply. Manifest the power that has been given to you. We are the instruments of Yahovah's glory to make miracles happen. All things must conform to the spoken word of Yahovah.

You have to work the dreams you have been given, or all you will have will be lost dreams that you never put to action to cause a change in your circumstances. Put your dreams and visions into action. Now is a good time; tomorrow might be too late. The time for a chance is coming to an end, then there will be no chances left at all.

All Yahovah wants you to give him is your heart. He is the one that will transform you and put you together his way.

JWG/His Way Miracle Healing Sanctuary

A CALL TO ALL TO WAKE UP

It is hereby proclaimed. This is a call to all to come back to their roots, the Living Word, and discard all religious vanities that have distorted the word of Yahovah, the Aleph Tau. They have distorted the word that was made flesh, Yahshua, by making what he came and created a vain religion instead of using their brains and thinking and reading and speaking the word. They are more worried about the footnotes, thinking somehow they will get out of it all, instead of enduring it and floating away like a fairy tale. They seek a sign from God to fit their own misguided hearts and minds because they wish not to use their brains and want a machine to think for them. They want to live in a box instead of out of the box, in Yahvah's Circle

Things have now changed, and you can no longer put me in the box of religion. I will not fit in any box you have prepared for me. I have created spheres that have no ends that circle spheres of fire.

You now live in a new age. Can you not see it? The good old boy network that got us here to begin with has and will come to an end. Why would the Lord want anyone saved at all if he was just going to destroy it all anyway? It would be pointless. So don't take what I say for granted till after you see the revival in action. It will be different than before, so many will not see it all at first or at all as before. So some could fall away because they could not look the other way. It has and will not happen as they were taught or thought it would be. It will be different than before, as I have always done before. Because it is a new time and a new day today and every day. That is the way I want it to be.

So be careful of the prophecy you accept and live by because you will have to live through that prophecy, good or bad, that you accepted as truth without finding confirmations in the spoken words of the Torah and in the

Bible. You were taught and accepted lies as truth because that is what you were taught as truth, but it was a lie. It has no scriptural basis. It is a theory that was taught as truth, that did not come to pass a thousand years ago and so will not come to pass now, unless you are brainwashed enough to let it or make it happen by going along with a lie. You were led to believe a theory from the footnotes that have no basis in the Torah. Just like any theory, it has come back to hit you in the face to make you lose the race. They think they know the truth, but they don't know the truth of the word at all, and they never will unless they give their hearts to me, Yahshua.

So you have people playing on the public's fears to see how they can benefit from the calamity they create from religious people's fears. Every end-time prediction has always turned out to be a false doctrinal disappointment with no basis in the actual word of Yahovah.

Too many people are more worried about their images. There is no end of time; there is always a new beginning, because the future is not set in stone. They have and are not walking and being in his image. I need to walk the way Yahshua walks all the time.

His eyes are your eyes. He likes to look at things through your eyes. He likes to speak through your mouth. Open it and speak the word. Speak in the power of the word of Yahovah. Manifest the power of Yahshua by the spoken word.

To know the word, you must speak the word, you must know the word to do the word. You must speak, read and know the word because he is the word. The word is the Torah, Yahshua, the Christ, is the living word of the Torah.

I have never sent any person that could not read and write the word, because to know the true word, you must be able to read and write the word, for he is the living word sent to all mankind. You must know the word to do the word. To know the word, you must speak the word. The Torah is the living word of Yahovah that has been given to mankind to supply all our needs through proper discipline and faith with action, which is contrary to false religious doctrines that are not based on the living word but are set up to control and manipulate people with doctrines that are not from the Lord Yahovah.

WAKE UP CALL

Do what the Living Word teaches. Do what Yahshua preaches. Do what the Holy Spirit of Yahovah teaches.

The word was meant to be spoken over and over and never changed or distorted to fir denominational religious false doctrines. Do greater works than he did, for you are a son of the living Yah, and you have the Holy Spirit. Teach love and not fear. Stay grounded on the solid rock. Get your eyes right on Yahshua. Yahovah needs your body to create miracles.

JWG 12/1/10

LET MY PEOPLE GO

מֵאֱלִשְׂרֹפ יב רֶהָ גּ לְפפּ יּמ תֹל

It is hereby proclaimed. "Let my people go. Let them go now," says the great I am. Let the people go from bondage. Let my people live free of governmental bondage and suppression.

If you want to harden your heart even harder like Pharaoh, I, the great I am, will make it even harder. Do not think like an Egyptian or Roman that did not know when to wake up from the coming disaster and stop it from happening.

Yahovah has put it in your hands to choose his way or some other false pathway. Beelzebub, you have kept many nations in bondage. It is now the time for you to let them all go. Even though Pharaoh and Caesar will not listen to anything anyway, you still must go and proclaim my words to Pharaoh and Caesar. In this way, I can show the world my miracles.

You have my people and nation in bondage. Let them go. Let them go, set them free from taxes and unpayable debt. Let them have their Promised Land free and clear. Take them out of bondage and set them free. Do not bind them with governmental dogmas and agendas that are not the will of the whole people but of the few that want to keep people in bondage to them forever.

All things must conform and are subject to the spoken word of Yahovah and the image of Christ. I have taken you from the house of the taskmaster and bondages into the land of paradise.

I command you in the name of Yahovah, let my people go. Free them now. It has been veiled to those who are perishing and blinded by the yahs of this world, the yah of the last dead age.

Now the new age has come upon us, but the living word, Yahshua, will make a light shine in their hearts and tear down the veil that has blinded them.

I command you all to be freed of all your bondages.

Let all my people go now. I have broken all your bindings with the hammer of the word. I have loosened your bindings with the power of the word. You are free now, disciple. You are justified by trusting in the living word of Yahovah.

Now you can and will receive the inheritance that I have stored up for you and your families, an everlasting inheritance that will last forever.

JWG/His Way Miracle Healing Sanctuary
1/1/11

REVEAL MY DESTINY! IT HAS BEEN REVEALED!

My destiny will be revealed before me. I hereby proclaim, nothing can stop me now, not even me. I will be allowed to fulfill my destiny. So help me, Yahovah, to fulfill it in every way. My destiny cannot be prolonged or stopped by anything any longer. Nothing can stop it from being fulfilled every day of my life.

I will have and have been given precisely the right instruments at precisely the right time to do the work of Yahovah. Yahovah will reveal it to me, as I need to know it, so I don't mess it up with my mouth.

I will have exactly what I need at exactly the right time to do the job I receive to do. Yahovah has preordained my destiny. He has revealed to me my destiny. He has prepared an unbroken path for me to accomplish exactly what I need to do for Yahovah today and every day of my life. "I, Yahovah, know every deed you have ever done or will do, every thought you ever made or will make."

My destiny will manifest before me daily, so I renew my mind daily. My life has been divinely orchestrated, and I was chosen by Yahovah to be on earth at this time in earth's history, to make a difference and make the right kind of change for Yahovah.

My life will now be manifested to a new level of my destiny. He has set me up to manifest his glory in me. My new level of destiny means a new level of obedience to Yahovah. I will, at precisely the right time, complete exactly what Yah wants me to complete. I will accomplish all tasks given daily easily at precisely the right time and without delay or trouble, I will rise here now and never fall from grace forever.

WAKE UP CALL

"I will now make you a legend forever. Because when I make a hero, they can never be stopped by anything at any time. They go anywhere and everywhere. I tell them to go. I tell them to move mountains, and they cannot be stopped because they have been sent by me, the Lord of all things, Yahovah. My protection is with them wherever they go or will go." They have a hedge of protection that can and will not be penetrated by anything anywhere at any time. We are the instruments that Yahovah uses to make miracles happen.

I thank you for fulfilling my destiny, oh Lord Yahovah, my strength. I love you, Yahovah, my high tower of defense. Yahovah has put the power into my hands to fulfill my destiny completely.

2/1/11 JWG

TO KNOW THE WORD

To say the word, you must know how to speak the holy word.
To speak the word, you must know the word.
To know the word, you must have a relationship with the Word.
To have a relationship with the Word, you must commune daily with the word.
To have a relationship with him means he knows you and you know him.
To know him is to love him.
To know him, you have to know the word.
To know the word is to do the word.
To know him is to do his word, and his word sets you free.

If you can't speak the word, then you can't say the word to know the word.

If you can't say the word, then you don't know the word and the word does not know you and you never will unless you give your heart to him.

But the word will make a light shine in their heart and tear down the veil that has blinded them with a rock.

Blessed is he that does not get offended at my word. It is veiled to those who are perishing and blinded by the god of this world, the god of the last age, not the new age to come.

2/8/11 JWG

I AM NAZIR
I AM A NAZARITE

I am a Nazarite. I walk the pathway chosen for me by Yahovah. Most humans will not walk this path with Yahovah, Yahshua, and the Holy Spirit.

I must walk the walk and not the talk before the one who comes again to ride in and walk his second walk. I have given my life to Yahovah forever. Now he lives inside me, and I in him. I have been separated unto him by taking the vow of the Nazir. Yah has accepted my petition and tested me to receive the gifting of the Nazarite. The locks of my hair shall grow long. My lips will not taste wine of grapes, and I will not touch a dead human being. I have always had. I have now gained and will always have the supernatural strength of Yahovah. He has empowered me with the strength of the Nazarite. I will raise the dead, cleanse those with sickness, and put my blessing on their heads forever. I have received my inheritance from Yahovah, and it will manifest in me daily.

Yahovah will bless and keep you in the palm of his hands. Yahovah will have favor upon you and bring you mercy. Yahovah will bring his countenance upon you. Yahovah will make his face shine upon you and be gracious to you and bring you peace. Yahovah's words will rest upon your lips all the days of your life. This is my dream, vision, and destiny, and I make the pathway out. I take a stand and cry out, "Make straight your pathway in front of Yahovah. Repent and become redeemed and give your heart to Yahovah. Do not shake hands with false religions that do not believe that I, Yahshua, am one with Yahovah. I am the living word made flesh."

I must always remind Yahovah to be patient with all of us, but his patience will wear thin one day.

JWG 2/13/11

TO MY APOSTLES IN TRAINING

פֿ מ׳ בֿסףל ּנ פֿח־נֲנֽ

You can be anywhere, and I, Yahovah, can pick you up and put a hat, suit, vest, tie, belt, and the weapons you will need on you. These are my garments of praise and worship to Yahovah, I can make you a real apostle and godfather, my son, and I will. You are not to think like a bum or act like one or dress like one. I did not wake you up for you to fall asleep again and become a pious, religious person who lives only to condemn and gossip about their fellow servants. You are to walk in love, not condemnation. Condemnation kills the spirit of love. Walking in love does not mean that I overlook my brother's mistakes for friendship.

The religious spirit kills your spiritual life and your spiritual walk with Yahovah. Yahovah is your best friend. Now act like he is. Do not walk in fear and cowardice; be bold, fearless, and courageous always. I, Yahovah, walk with you now and always. The fire that I throw you in is very hot, and it will bring out all the dross. I do not lie; neither should you. I will fulfill all things that I have promised in my own time, not yours. It's not always going to be fun and easy. Sometimes it will be the hardest thing you have ever done. I have to take you through certain things to train you and keep you weary of or from being led by other people or sexes that are only worried about their own interests and they do not hear from the Lord and will not as long as they operate in fear and deceit.

I, Yahovah, must lead you alone, and no one else or nothing else can. I may cause you to fall in love and then lose it to find it again. This is in order to show your mind how the indwelling of the spirit works and to show you I will always love you more than anyone else. I will never stop loving you, says the Lord. I have given you gifts that will only come to fruit after going through the trials I send your way to overcome. Even though they have been given to you at birth, the trial brings it to fruit in the right season. There are certain things you can only do yourself to have to overcome it. I have been with you since birth, and I will always walk with you. I have given you one legion of Holy Spirit-filled angels trained for service to Yahovah to help you complete the work given to you by Yah. You are a general in my army of saints. Act like it and tell them what to do in tongues for all things needed supernaturally. If it is possible, you will hear in the spirit "It is done." They are subject to the Trinity, you, and me. They are subject to you under certain guidelines they will set the parameters of. This process is to help you attain greater trust and faith in Yah. To get you to believe and think in the spirit, hear in the spirit, walk in the spirit, and see in the spirit. They are to help and guide you through the narrow pathways of my discipleship and training.

The pressure you feel upon you is not crushing you. It is the pressure of the refining fires that are turning you into a diamond with a rainbow inside. We are all put to the test, and that testing never comes the way we want it to come. It's a test you will pass one day.

Beauty for ashes, refining through brokenness-this is how I, Yahovah, put you back together in the way I want you to be better than when I found you and picked you up.

The world's order will always seek to pull you back into disbelief and rebellion, to take you from where you are supposed to be in the spirit to a place that you are not supposed to be. It's easy to be a critic. It's hard to be a true leader of men. Power is an addiction that must be released in order to cure it, especially when it is time to be released from power or to delegate powers to be released to others.

You are now at the right place at the right time. At this place, you are being fed a steak and not a baby bottle. It is better that you make the youth your family for now, because your destiny lies in teaching the youth to respect the liberties they have and to know all things are possible to those who believe. We must start teaching what to do and how to get there.

I want to see miracles again, as in the new days to come, not the old ones of the past. This is what I, Yahovah, want to see. You are a priest of the new covenant priesthood, which is a priest of a new order after Abraham and Melchizedek, different from those that you have been taught to religiously practice. I want your heart, not your religion. Carry my cross-and no other religion. My blood, body, and Holy spirit, which is my new covenant with you, has made all things clean, even you. Forever.

The word of the Lord Yahovah, from James Garner.

JWG AEP 2/20/11

YOU ARE MY DISCIPLE
לְפִּסֹ֫ד

You are saints that I have dressed and fully clad in wolves' clothing with the heart of the lamb of Yah and the indwelling of his Holy Spirit.

You do not stand out. You fit right in where I send you, whatever I send you to do, and wherever you go.

You follow me of your own free will. You have given me your whole undivided heart because you know I am the Christ, son of the living Yah.

You will not have to worry or carry many vestments, because I can and will sustain you through all the storms forever and ever.

You will carry my vestments of praise, and they will bestow my power upon you wherever your journey is.

You will journey easily to all the places I have sent you, and that dwelling place will sustain you and all that are journeying with you while you are there.

You are my disciple, and you will follow no one else's teachings.

You can only worship Yahovah and him alone. Nothing in heaven or earth you may worship but Yahovah and him alone.

You will follow his son, Yahshua, and him alone you will follow.

You will follow no new teaching but Yahshua's.

You will follow no new religion or old one. I have promised you a new thing and not an old one.

You have been filled with the Holy Spirit.

You will listen to the Lord's guidance and teachings and accept no new ones.

You will follow only Yahovah and his son, Yahusa, alone, and no other yahs do you worship or follow.

You will have me, Yahovah, go before you and prepare the way I have sent you to go. If you have gone astray, I will send a shepherd to guide you back home.

You have been chosen for all the tasks given to you. Act like it. You are to bring together the lost and make disciples of Yahshua the Christ, not followers of you.

You are to walk in love and grace, knowing the right time to act always.

You do not walk in condemnation, because condemnation kills and the spirit brings the love of life.

You and I are one, clothed in vestments of power and now very dangerous and unstoppable.

You and I will walk in unity of spirit and love always.

You will speak it into existence by faith, trusting the Lord to do it.

You are made whole through me, free from anxiety and fear, ready for maximum potential increase. My body and blood have made you whole. My body and blood that was shed for you and all humanity have purified you and made you whole. Do this in remembrance of me only.

You have been redeemed by the sacrifice of Yahshua and are a new Holy Spirit-filled being in Christ.

You follow me in discipline and love, because you have willingly Given me you whole heart.

You will spend time with me daily and become wise and successful, full of knowledge and peace.

You will repent of all sins daily.

You will remove all fear, pain, and sickness and heal the sick of all diseases.

You will cast out and into Sheol all demonic and unclean spirits.

You will trample down all false religious doctrines and all doctrines of the Antichrist.

You will have the power to overcome all the works of Beelzebub and his false teachers and prophets.

You will have no poison harm you.

You will have your strength be renewed daily by the indwelling of the Holy Spirit.

WAKE UP CALL

You will be transformed into the image of the Christ Yahshua.
You will have the power to prosper and have my favor on you always.
You will rise up and be a person of honor, excellence, and integrity.
You will always stand before me whole and blameless in love.
You predestined us to be adopted as your sons and daughters.
You loved me and knew me before I was born again.
You will come in my name, Yahshua, and my name alone.
You will walk with me forever and ever, and I will be you only Yah.
You will always be with me, I will never leave you or forsake you.

You are my sons and daughters and you know how dearly and deeply I love you always. Choose to honor Yah as a servant to him and his new kingdom to come.

JWG 4/1/11, His Way Miracle Healing Sanctuary
Word received by James W. Garner, president and founder

THE COMING OF THE NEW KINGDOM

דִנָּה תָּ כָּ הִ־שַׁחֲ־יָ טָ מֻדֻעַבְּ תַּ הַת טָ נֻפְמַשַ וַח

The coming of the new kingdom of Yahovah is hereby proclaimed. The coming of the new kingdom of Yahovah is at hand. I seek new stewards in my new kingdom that has come. The old kingdom is passing away, and the new kingdom has come. The old guard must change hands with the new guard of stewards of my new kingdom to come.

These are the days I made for you and you were born again for, to rule and reign in my new kingdom for one thousand years. Those who wish to continue in the old traditions of men, following the spirit of religiosity instead of the spirit of truth, they will be given no quarter. No mercy will be shown to them, for they have again denied my deity to my face yet again to follow another vain religion. The open doorway will be shut.

To those who wish to innocently kill the innocent, they will be found guilty by my decree. Murder of the innocent in the name of God, but not by my name or by my spoken words, will suffer my wrath, sentences, and judgments, and the spirit of death will remove them and all their seed from the earth forever, for it is subject to me, Yahovah, and the Trinity, and it wanders the earth, ready to consume those who will not repent of their old traditions of men that I have not set up nor do I acknowledge. All their works will be thrown in the fires of hell.

I set up my only begotten Son, my living word, and it alone for you to follow. The living word cannot be contained within a book. I did not set up religiosity for you to follow. Men set up these religious rules that I, Yahovah, did not require of you to do. Nor do I want you to practice them. I, Yahovah, do not send illiterate teachers to you. I never have, and I never will. I do not and will not continue to allow these false teachers to persist in murdering the innocent in the name of Baal (Allah), the curse.

I do not teach you prayers that you cannot read or write or fully understand. I told you to pray in tongues if you don't know what to pray every day. All I have asked of you is your undivided heart. You must be able to read the word of Yahovah to know Yahshua. You must be able to write the word so you can pass on the word. You must live the word every day, not one day a week. Yahshua is the living word, and there is no other. No earthly human can or could fulfill the true word of Yahovah as perfectly as Yahshua has and will again.

The teachings of Yah are not to control you but to give you access to the spirit world around you that you cannot normally see or sense. Vain repetition of religious acts is as the stench of rotten vinegar to me. It is the new wine that the religious have been putting in old wineskins instead of new ones, trying to hold on to something that has and must be given away to all others chosen by Yahovah.

I do not want you to believe in me simply because you have heard of me or read about me, but because I know you and you know me as your Yah and friend. I have given to all the free will to choose any pathway they choose with or without me. You must repent daily, or you are in denial. You must walk with me, not without me. You must follow me and me alone, not every doctrine that blows your way. I am the only gateway to the Father. I am your only savior; the law cannot save you. You can only enter the kingdom of Yah one way, his way, through him alone and no other way.

When I come, all the angels in the heavens will come with me. All the dead living spirits in Christ will follow behind me. All of Sheol, Beelzebub, and all who follow this loser will be subject to me and will do my bidding. The gates of hell have fallen down with a mighty crash. There will be nowhere you can hide from my army and me to come. Your kingdom has fallen down, and I am now taking over.

Beelzebub, your time has come to be chained in the pit of Sheol, and all of my armies and I will be able to watch you burn, burn, burn, and be extinguished from existence forever. You, your seed, and all who follow you and your seed will cease to exist for eternity, and you will be removed from existence forever. There will be nothing you can do to stop me or that will stop my wrath upon you and all who followed you. I will not forgive you of your blasphemy against Yahovah and the new kingdom to come. I am the risen Yahshua, the Christ. I will walk into my new kingdom to come as I walked everywhere during my life as a human on earth. As I have walked with Yahovah for my entire existence, it would be a sin for me to ride in on a horse. I was crucified for riding in on an ass.

My armies will walk into their own inheritance of the new kingdom. My armies have risen and are rising from their graves to conquer the earth and subdue the enemies of Yahovah. We will praise Yahovah everywhere we go, always moving forward, always taking ground, unstoppable by any opposing forces. I am coming sooner than you think. Beware I come with blazing fire in my eyes and the judgments of Yahovah on my lips. Act as if you expect me to. Be prepared for me to return with a new outcome. I will not relent. I hereby proclaim.

JWG 7/10/11, His Way Ministries

I, YASHUA, WILL WALK INTO THE PROMISE LAND

ד׃'ל דִּסָמוֹפ הָח תֵּנ כָּל'ִנ לִלנ זָהסה׃

I will walk into the new kingdom to come, the new Promised Land of your inheritance. I will walk through the east gate that has been shut and open it. I will set all this age's captives free. I will resurrect the dead. I will judge the quick and the dead. I will tear down the walls of religion. I will walk through the streets of Jerusalem. I will come in the name of Yahovah with my Father's armies. They will walk with me, and all the armies of the heavens will follow behind me and me alone, and we will walk all over every other army. I will walk on the temple mount and tear down the false religious idles of worship and walk all over them. I will dance through the new temple in Jerusalem. I will sing a new song. I will remove the Antichrist and all the false prophets and all who work for him. They will all cease to exist forever. I will establish the house of the Lord Yahovah forever. I will establish Yahovah's everlasting kingdom to come that will have no end, forever. I will reign over the new kingdom forever. I will do it the way Yahovah wants it done forever.

JWG 7/19/11

THE LAW AND THE SPIRIT
תָה ל־ּו ־נִד תֹה סְפִרְֹת

The law and the spirit do not walk together. The law brings death and judgement. The spirit brings life and redemption. The law tells you that you don't need Yah to do miracles, because somehow you have made yourself believe you're blessed by following religious rules I never gave for you to follow without me.

You are not to do as the heathen and worship idols to make a show out of my commands, to milk the poor of their money and keep them in slavery to a religion. But even now, they have no understanding of me in their heart, because they never gave it to me. They gave it to the law, thinking their works would get them there. You will always break the law when you walk by the spirit because you need miracles to walk by the spirit. You need the law to enslave men into false worship of idols. Even the worship of the law itself is a sin. You cannot mingle the two together and think somehow you have become sinless and not guilty. There is a big difference between walking in the right path and knowing the right path personally.

You have used mixed words of wisdom to mislead the masses. I have always said, follow me, not the law, not Judaism, not Islam- not any other Yah but me. What a shame on you all, you wealthy fake bastards of the Torah. You have milked my people for profit with a bunch of false prophets, thinking no one has seen, but I, Yahovah, see all things and have seen it all and have even written it in a book for you to see, just like the law book you love so much.

JWG 10/10/11

I AM A WARRIOR! I AM A WARRIOR IN THE ARMY OF MY YAH!

The great I Am is the supreme commander. The Holy Spirit-filled Bible is the word of Yah and our code of conduct. Wisdom is my teacher. The Holy Spirit is my guide and resides within me, giving me the same power as our Lord Yah. Worship, prayer, the spoken word in faith, and the word of our Lord Yah are my weapons of warfare. I have been trained by the Holy Spirit, taught by experience, tested by adversity, and tried by the fire of Yah.

I have been enlisted of my own free will in the special forces of the army of our living Yah, the Christ Jesus. Before I was born, I was selected for this task in the end times and have been enlisted for eternity. Christ enlisted and redeemed us with his blood. I will live and die in this army. I will never forget where I came from and how Christ and the Holy Spirit have changed me forever. I am capable, faithful, reliable, and dependable and able to complete any task given. If my Yah needs me, I am there. He can use me to complete any task given. I am a warrior! I am a leader! I am not a baby!

I do not need to be prepared, petted, primed up, pumped up, picked up, or pepped up! I am a knight in the army of my Yah. No one has to call me, remind me, write me, visit me, entice me, or lure me. I am a warrior! I am always prepared and in place to do any job called to do. I am a special forces' warrior! I am a committed disciple. I have no feelings to hurt. Nothing can stop me or turn me around. I cannot be discouraged enough to turn back from the mission given. I cannot lose anything. I came with nothing. I am not a quitter. I am a warrior! I will win all the battles I undertake! Our Yah supplies all my needs! I am more than a conqueror! I will always triumph! I can do all things through Christ who strengthens me!

Satan can't defeat us! Demons must run from us! Religious people can't put a blanket on us! Or disillusion us! The Antichrist can't stop me! Hell is afraid of me and can't handle me! I am a disciplined warrior, and death has no hold on me! Death cannot overtake me! No curse can affect me! All curses are broken in my path!

I present the power of the infinite living Yah! And all the created things must obey my words.

I am a special forces' warrior in Christ's army. I am advancing claiming territory.

I will not give up!

I will not retreat!

I am a warrior ever marching forward, forever taking ground till I'm heaven bound!

If Yahshua was walking on earth today starring in your eyes would he find 12 good men to follow him?

Here I stand during the course of battle. Will you stand with me?

Unless You Are Born Again

נִ֫־גִ־ נרבּ֗ רִ־ י֔ ססלנ֔

Unless you are born again, you cannot understand or experience The New Kingdom of heaven at all. Unless you are born again, you will not receive The Holy Spirit. Unless you are born again, you are still guilty and cannot see The Kingdom of heaven. Unless you are born again, I will not accept you into The New Kingdom on earth or in heaven. Unless you are born again, you cannot be my son or daughter because you cannot hear my voice. Unless you are born again, you will be judged guilty. Unless you are born again, you cannot see the true living word of Christ. Unless you are born again, you will waste your time on religion instead of a relationship with Yahovah!

JWG
8//21/11

The Adamic Alphabet

מלאסףPsalm 119 ףסאלמ
The Hebrew and American Alphabet

כטחזוהדגבא‎ תשׁרקצפסנמלכיטחזוהדגבא חשׁרקצפסנמלכיטחזוהדגבא

All reality is consequently compromised in the circular rotation sequence of which, A and T, these two letters form the beginning and the end of the essence of the alphabetical circle or order. this beginning was nothing; the end must therefore be also nothing, but nothing in its previous expansion of the circle or order the essence of a symbol is that it should convey to each person as much meaning as study and resident brainpower will enable them to grasp. The alphabet, in its higher aspect, is the record in symbols of what man has discovered about, what his relationship is to the universe of Yahovah. The alphabet was and is designed, to stimulate reflection and meditation on the word of Yahovah. The alphabet of Yahovah, enlightens the spirit of the individual of his or her own higher far-reaching heritage to Yahovah and that of all humans and all other intelligent forms of life are evidence of humankind's living bond with all of life, which is the unified brotherhood of the universal order of Yahovah, a royal priesthood of sons after the order of hero priests and the line of Melchizedek. Ranked not from lineage but, having the rank only from the heavenly father, Yahovah Adonia, to give you the rank of kingship, having your beginning and your end set and made unto you as a chosen son and high priest of Yahovah, abiding in him as a high priest continually forever. The special nature of Yahovah is his essence that flows freely threw out the whole universe. It represents the human entirety of existence. The letter "A" symbolizes the divine energy that preceded the initiated creation by the seeding power that existed before any other form could be realized to exist. So then, nothing can not work for you in the new kingdom of Yahovah outside the unconditional love of the kingdom of Yahvah, so to produce the power of Yahvah and his kingdom on earth, I must stay in the center of his circle of love and grace for all things melt in the presence of Yahovah's love. so out of the love and grace of Yahvah comes the power of Yahvah, for this is the foundation of his truth 'he that does not know how to love Yahvah with their whole heart does not know Yahvah'!

A = א
= (*ALEPH*, *ALEF*, ALPHA)

א = A = *alef* = #1 = air = with
= the clown = the joker
= the jester – the fool
= essence = brain waves = yoke
= wild = courage = ecstasy
= new birth = zero = ox
= the trump = trumpet = horn
= the state of no fear / no pain
= beginning and end
= the universal principle of realization that is experienced before the birth of after the death of a person, place, or thing and its renewal and or rebirth.

The first letter has always been the letter *a* and has always made the [ah] and [a] sound fundamental to human speech meaning *ox* and/or *ox yoke*.

A, or *alef,* could also be used to signify the numeral 1 and 0 once the word or Bible became to be interpreted legalistically instead of spiritually, removing words, letters, and names out of fear and of men and slavery, not Yahovah.

A is the symbol of Yahovah's universal order and cosmic unity and priesthood established by Adam, Enoch, Noah, Abraham, Aaron, Moshe, Melchizedek, Yahshua, Johanna, Paul and Mary, and others, and twenty-four heroes of this order will come and establish the new kingdom on earth as it is in heaven.

The letter *a* enjoys a philosophical glory, symbolizing the divine energy that preceded the initiated creation by this seeding power that existed before any other form could be realized and which is why the opening word of Genesis 1:1 starts with the word *bereshith* ("in the beginning"), which is the second letter in the alphabet. Because of this, *a* becomes the number 0, and the letter *b* becomes the number 1 legalistically.

So then correspondingly, *alef* represents a person's readiness to act, while *beth* represented and is imagined as the doer of things or the open door to my house. It also represents the creative power of giving birth

> ~to birth new life forms from a state of anticipation, freedom, and abundance, rather than from state of fear, poverty, and slavery,
>
> ~to give birth from the heart of Yahovah new ideas and new ways of thinking;
>
> ~to give birth from the body and blood of Christ to new ways of living in healthiness, fitness, and happiness;
>
> ~to give birth from the Holy Spirit new ways of transforming into your destiny and God-given potential;
>
> ~to give birth from Christ's love, passion, and sensitivity in everything you do and say;
>
> ~to give birth from our God-given spiritual gifting to new ways of setting limits on vulture-like people or situations;
>
> ~to give birth to not bearing the burdens of others we were not meant to bare;

~to give the birth from our position in Christ inspired vision and energy and a creative vision of original and innovative ideas and thoughts;

~to give birth from out place of rest in Christ calmness and gentleness to new forms of ideas that will unify relationships with energy and vision.

The root of the powers of the air invoked force as opposed to natural force, whirling energy, activity, and strength through declared force, as affirmation of justice, upholding divine authority for conquest of new kingdom.

The clown unifies thoughts with energy and vision to create original and innovative ideas that are not based on feelings but are based on real solutions. The clown uses his multiple talents to generate abundance and fruitfulness in everything he does. He wears the Christ's belt of truth and so is committed to bringing creativity into solid usable matter in truth and fact.

Air or wind symbolizes the mode of mental transmissions or the internal output of the brain's electrical circuitry.

The clown represents the ecstatic adventure of growing and unfolding in our own journey of the hero and our true destiny in life, walking with Christ Yahshua.

The character of the man living in the word is happiness, ox head, horn, the word of Yahvah.

> Happy are those whose lives are faultless, who live according to the word of Yahovah. Happy are those who follow his commands, who obey him with all their heart. They never do wrong; they walk in Yahovah's ways. Yahovah you have given us your commandments and told us to obey them faithfully. (Psalm 119:1-8)

How I hope I will be faithful in keeping your instructions! If I pay attention to all your commandments, then I will not be put to shame. As I learn your righteous judgments, I will praise you with a clean heart.

WAKE UP CALL

I will obey your word, because you will never abandon me!

בבבבבבבבבבבבבבבב

B = בּ
= (BET, BAYT, BETH, BETA)

בּ = B = *bet* = #2 = Mercury

= the magician – the musician

= the juggler = the performer

= the inner body – the artist

= balance timing = dwelling

= communication = the house

=cleansing the house = sound

= refining = purification = tent

= in the beginning = *bereshith*

= the doer of things = doer

= the universal principle of communication that is balanced, healing, and transformative. It represents the sound *b* and a house to dwell in.

    This letter has always represented the first number and the second letter even though the letter *a* was the first letter given to humans by Yahovah.
    This is why the Bible starts with letter *b* and the phrase in *the beginning*, or *bereshith*, and the reason why the word oh Yahovah originally started with the letter *a*, which was the first graven image falsely worshipped by the Semites or Hebrews, a bull or calf.

It represents the first and second commandments from Yahvah: "You will worship me and me alone, and no other Yah will you worship, for I am a jealous Yah and I will not tolerate halfheartedness."

In science, it represents second place in context with its brother alpha.

It represents that your body is God's house, and your house is his house in balance and prepared as a pure balanced dwelling place.

It represents the power of communication that is impartial and balanced toward each every one.

It represents communication that is inspired, resilient, and well timed in action and preparation.

The artist has ten tools in his hands or toolbox, and he always picks the appropriate tools for the job required:

1. *The coin.* It represents the ability to communicate wealth in ways that can and will assist finances and investments.
2. *The kerub.* It represents communication that is like a light or lantern that lights the genius of the mind and the pathway to take.
3. *The phoenix.* It is the wand or rod in the artist's hand that enables you to communicate from a philosophical and spiritual base.
4. *The arrow.* It represents direct, honest, truthful, and straightforward communication.
5. *The winged eye.* It represents the symbol of inspired vision that is true, clear, and articulate.
6. *The scroll or book.* It represents the power of communication that is written, drawn, built, painted, or sculpted that is inspired, artistic, transformative, and imaginative.
7. *Wigged egg.* It represents communication that is prompted from our essence, then it is formed and delivered or birthed.
8. *The cup with coiled snake.* It represents the power to communicate the full range of one's feelings without color blindness.
9. *The sword.* It represents the weapon that gives you the ability to cut through old religious dogmas and thought patterns to articulate new ideas and thoughts clearly and concisely from Yahovah.

10. *The golden ape.* It represents wisdom that is flexible, awake, and aware of all communication lines available to complete the job given.

It is the capacity to be able to communicate equally artistically, orally and/ or written.

It represents the wisdom, the will, the word, and the logos by whom the worlds were created and the energy was sent forth.

~ The manifestation in action of the idea of the Father in heaven ~
~ The staff of Moshe (Moses) ~
~ The creative force in action ~
~ The character of the man in the word, cleansing the inner soul or inner house ~
~ Cleansing man's house ~the house~
~ Obedience to the word of Yahvah ~

> How can a young person live a pure life? By obeying your word, with all my heart I try to serve you. Don't let me break your commands; I have taken your words to hearts so I would not sin against you. Yahvah should be praised.
>
> Teach me your demands. My lips will tell about all the words you have spoken. I enjoy living by your word as people enjoy great riches. I think about your orders and study your ways I enjoy obeying your demands, and I will not forget your word. (Psalm 119:9-16)

WAKE UP CALL

גגגגגגגגגגגגגגגגגגגגגגגגגגגגגגג

G, C = ג
= (GIMEL, GAMMA)

ג = G = *gimel* = #3 = moon = waves
= the high priestess = nature
= instinct = perception
= the sixth sense = intuition
= self-trust = discernment
= liberty = freedom = liberate
= self-resourcefulness
= throwing stick = camel hump
= boomerang = camel
= the universal principle of intuition, independence, self-trust, and self-resourcefulness

This letter originally had the *g*, gamma sound, and was later moved and changed to the *c* sound.

It is a reminder that we are not to sacrifice our strengths for quietness or our gentleness for our strength.

It is a commitment to have equal balance in gentleness and strength.

Our intuition has three aspects that are present at each level of our consciousness:

1). Intellectual intuition (mental)
2). Divine intuition (spiritual)
3). Corporal intuition (physical)

It represents the resourcefulness and the capacity to go a long journey and always find the oasis, a state of synchronization and self-determination, how the word will enlighten the spirit.

~ camel's hump ~ throwing stick ~
~ happiness in the word of Yahvah ~

> Be good to me your servant so I may live and obey your teachings. Open my eyes so I will see the wonderful truth in your word. I am here on earth for just a little while; do not hide your commands from me. My heart aches with longing; I want to know your judgments at all times. You reprimand the proud; cursed are those who don't follow your commands. Free me from their insults and scorn, because I have kept your word. The rulers meet and plot against me, but I will study your teachings. Your instructions give me pleasure; they are my advisers. (Psalm 119:17-24)

דדדדדדדדדדדדדד

D = ד
= (DALET, DA 'LETH, DELTA)

ד = D = *dalet* = #4 = Venus
= fleur-de-lis = the empress
= love with understanding
= salt = creative rule = beauty
= inspired power = true love
= worship with wisdom = way in
= the open door = entrance
= door = the gatekeeper
= the universal principle of love with wisdom

This letter took the sound *d* as our *d* still does, which always meant "open door."
In math, *d* represents the increment of change in a series.
In science, *d*, or delta, represents and/or means a triangular shape or triangle.
It represents the state of love and/or true love.

~ true love (soul mate) ~

~ agape (mutual) ~

~ philleo (brotherly) ~

~ paterno (paternal) ~

It is the love, beauty, and creative power of the feminine magnetic nature that is true. It represents the balanced, trusting heart rather than the protective, controlling heart.

It represents giving in equal propositions to the capacity to receive.

It represents you are as comfortable giving love as receiving love, the complete ability to extend love and receive love.

It is the power of yin energy.

It is a reminder that when we approach life from an attitude of love combined with wisdom, we will resist the need to overgive or push to make things happen spiritually, emotionally, and physically; nor will we protect or hold ourselves back spiritually, emotionally, or physically.

It is the capacity to give mentally, emotionally, physically, and spiritually in all the appropriate proportions needed.

It represents the healing power of love that is nurturing, comforting, and supportive.

It represents the mind and the heart having equal balance and proportion.

It represents spiritual messages that have been recognized and/ or brought into spiritual awareness.

It reminds us that wisdom is within us; therefore, you must listen to your inner guidance.

It represents transforming our underdeveloped parts to awaken to who we are in Christ.

It represents looking and seeing with diverse forms of perception.

It illustrates the magnetic pull of the feminine nature within us and its necessity to offer love with wisdom.

Going through the door of Yah's word will sustain all needs.

~ Open door ~

The word is an open door.

~ A door ~

~ Determination to obey the word of Yahvah ~

As I lie defeated in the dust; revive me, as you have promised.
I confessed all I have done, and you answered me; teach me your ways.
Help me to understand your word, and I will meditate on your wonderful teachings.
I am overcome by sorrow; strengthen me, as you have promised.
Keep me from going the wrong way and in your goodness teach me your word.
I have chosen to be obedient; I have paid attention to your judgments.
I have followed your instructions, Yahovah; do not let me be put to shame.
I will eagerly obey your word, because you will give me more understanding. (Psalm 119:25-32)

הההההההההההההההההההה

H, E = ה
= (HE, HAY, HEH)

ה = H = heh = #5 = Aquarius = lilac
= amethyst = the star = purple
= the water bearer = grace
= internal guidance = beauty
= heliotrope = time porthole
= window of grace = window
= child of my strength = gap
= tribe of Benjamin = kindness
= guiding light = refinement
= picture = surprise = banner
= jump = image = representation
= the universal principle of self-independence, self-reliance, and self-confidence

The star is Aquarius.
It represents the symbol of the groundbreaking, inventive, and creative mind.
Today *he* has become our letter *e*, still the fifth letter, while *khet* has supplied our *h*, the eighth letter.
The *he* illustrates a person's shout of surprise, which sounded like our *hey*. The letter once carried the *he* sound and then became the *e* sound by 800 BC.

A human being is not an ape, an animal, a thing, or a process, but an opening through which Yahovah can manifest.

It represents the guiding light, the star of David, the star of Christ Yahshua, the star of Bethlehem.

It is the quality of looking within to find the truth and trusting the inner sixth sense within us to give us a guiding light in the darkness.

It is the state of radiance and confidence that is neither inflated nor deflated but balanced in truth and love.

Deep confidence is the ability to confide in and trust oneself, which allows us to fully express ourselves to the full extent of our abilities and talents.

When we trust our inner guidance, we see things more clearly and become more spontaneous, like flowing water, with our approach instead of being a stagnant pond.

The sparkle and confidence in our inherent life force that has every intention of actualizing all creative ideas on earth through our own kingdom natures.

It reminds each of us we are an opening for Yahvah to manifest the guiding light and power of Yahvah through our self-respect, which has three components. We are able to unfold like flowers and grow more fully into our many-colored expression of Christ.

The word makes us see what the word is doing on the earth.

~ porthole in time ~ the window ~

~ grace window ~

Yahvah will give you eyes to see and ears to hear so that you will be strong as you stand for righteousness.

A Prayer for Understanding

Teach me, Yahovah, the meaning of your commandments, and I will obey them at all times.

Explain your word to me, and I will obey it; I will keep it with all my heart.

Keep me obedient to your commandments, because in them I find happiness.

Give me the desire to obey your word rather than be rich.

Keep me from paying attention to what is worthless; be good to me, as you have promised.

Keep your promise to me, your servant –the promise you make to those who obey you.

Save me from the insults I fear; how wonderful are your judgments!

I want to obey your word; give me new life, for you are righteous. (Psalm 119:33–40)

ווווווווווווווווווווווווווווווווו

W, U = ו

= (VAV, WAW, VAU, WOW)

ו = W = *vav* = #6 = Taurus = rule

= diamond/amber = supremacy

= blue and gold = prosperity

= the hierophant = ancestors

= wisdom = teaching = bull

= faith = bracket = collection

= tribe of Manasseh = power

= choosing to forget = nail

= peg in a hole = plug opening

= the universal principle of education and knowledge that is experienced in our life and our families that requires us to trust our faith in Yahvah

This letter in the Hebrew and Phoenician dialect took the w sound exemplified in the start of the letter's name and became the *f* sound in English.

The letter *u* was moved to the twenty-third letter by the Greeks and called upsilon.

Faith is asked for in all parts of our individual experiences, and yet the test of faith is often challenged and experienced most often within family situations.

It represents the use of perception that requires wisdom and instinct without second-guessing the situation.

It represents to have or obtain awareness by the use of all the senses, to discern, know, or understand.

It represents how to apply the sanctified and divine to the external world.

It represents how to put into form the internal and external for practical use.

The bull reminds us to implement and take action on our ideas and bring them into form.

The lion reminds us of the expansive and unlimited creativity that waits to be utilized.

The man reminds us of our desire to be original.

The eagle reminds us to follow what has spirit and significance for our lives.

The eagle (commitment), the man (originality and vision), the bull (practicality), the lion (creativity)-these are the four aspects of faith.

They represent the concepts needed to handle change.

True salvation only comes by the word of Yahovah.

- the peg in hole – plug the opening -

The days of lack are coming to an end, and Yahvah will bring wealth and prosperity to your house.

~ peg / nail ~

~ trusting the word of Yahvah ~

> Show me how much you love me Yahovah, and save me according to your promise.
>
> Then I can answer those who insult me because I trust in your word.
>
> Enable me to speak the truth at all times, because my hope is in your judgments.
>
> I will always obey your word, forever and ever.

I will live in perfect freedom because I try to obey your teachings.

I will announce your plans to kings and I will not be ashamed.

I find pleasure in obeying your commands.

I respect and love your commandments; I will meditate on your instructions. (Psalm 119:41–48)

ךךךךךךךךךךךךךךךךךךךךךךךךך

Z, G = ז

= (ZAYIN, ZAIN)

ז = Z = zayin = #7 = Gemini = love

= emerald = bright green

= the lovers = the twins

= the capability of interaction

= alignment = agree = harmony

= tribe of Rueben = alliance

= my child of revelation = ax

= sword = weapon = hammer

= the universal principle of aptitude and dexterity for interaction in relations with contacts, associates, acquaintances, friends, family, animals, and the earth,

It represents in every relationship, whether it be friend, family member, an animal, a colleague, or a deep loved one, You must have childlike innocence, curiosity and playfulness, loyalty and commitment, and the gift of spaciousness, the allowing of space for contemplation, introspection, and the need to be alone, which is necessary for any relationship to stay blessed, awake, and alive.

It represents the union of two opposites to create unity.

~ Salt and sulfur ~

The sword represents the intellectual process that takes place in the uniting of two opposite elements.

It represents, when two are at one in their innermost hearts, they shatter the strength of iron or bronze; and when two understand each other in their innermost hearts, their words are sweet and strong. Like the fragrance of orchids.

It represents that the Creator blesses this deliberate synthesis.

There are nine kinds of love:

1.) Love for Yahovah, Yahshua, and the Holy Spirit
2.) Love between husband and wife
3.) Love between parent and children
4.) Love for servant to master
5.) Love between friend and friend
6.) Love that is passionate and illicit
7.) Love of an animal, place, or thing that has served as a friend, companion, and servant
8.) Love of an idol
9.) Love of a man, machine, animal, or thing more than God

Love has many forms, from one extreme to another, from passion to compassion. It represents to us the different kinds of relationship lines or the different kind of bonding that we can experience in our lives and the responsibilities incurred with each new relationship.

The I Ching says, "Even a single passion still lurking in the heart has power to obscure reason."

Passion and reason cannot exist side by side. Therefore, fighting without quarter is necessary, if the good is to prevail. In a resolute struggle of good against evil, there are, however, definite rules that must be discarded if good is to succeed.

1.) First, resolution must be based on a union of strength and friendliness.
2.) Second, a compromise with evil is not possible; evil must under all circumstances be openly discredited. Nor must our passion or shortcomings be glossed over.

3.) Third, the struggle must not be carried on directly by force. If evil is branded, it thinks of weapons, and if we do it in the favor of fighting against it blow by blow, we lose in the end, because thus we ourselves get entangled in hatred and passion. Therefore, it is important to begin at home, to be on guard in our own person against the faults that we have branded. In this way, finding no opponent, the sharp edges of the weapons of evil become dulled. For the same reasons, we should not combat our faults directly. As long as we wrestle with them, they continue to be victorious. So we fight in grace.

4.) Forth, and final resolution, the best way to overcome and fight evil is to make energetic progress in the good.

In times of darkness, it is important that we trust our intuition and that we have the right attitudes in our beliefs and in our thinking.

In times of positivity, it is important to follow what has heart and meaning and that we also, through our actions and behavior, implement what has passion and heart for us.

All relationships require us to be creative.

All relationships require that we clear our loyalties and priorities.

All relationships are a transformative experience so that physically in relationships, we change and transform and let go of old identities.

Each relationship has an internal or spiritual connection.

It reminds us that fundamental sincerity is the only proper basis for forming relationships of any kind.

It represents the principle of duality (yin and yang) within our nature and the dynamic and magnetic or light and dark within our nature.

The sword of the word cut unbelief from my life.

The word of Yahvah is my weapon.

The word is my sword.

Yahvah will cause things to come into alignment in your life and use you for his kingdom's work.

It represents confidence in the word of Yahvah.

> Remember your promise to me, your servant; it
> has given me hope. Even in my suffering I was

comforted because you're promise gave me life. The proud are always scornful of me but I have not departed from your word. I remember your judgments of long ago, and they bring me comfort, o Yahvah ! When I see the wicked breaking the law I am filled with anger. During my brief earthly life I compose songs about your commands. In the night I remember you Yahovah, and I think about your word. I find my happiness in obeying your commands. (Psalm 119:49-56)

חחחחחחחחחחחחחחחחחחחח

CH, J = ח
= (HET, CHETH, KHET)

ח = Ch, j = *het* = #8 = cancer
= crab = barrier = wall
= alexandrite/moonstone
= the chariot = change = pi
= transform = purple/gold
= obedience to the word
= double portion = a fence
= tribe of Ephraim = hedge
= *x* marks the spot = field
= boundary line = enclosure
= the universal principle of change, motion, and movement

Originally sounding *ch* like in *Bach*. As with all the early letters, the sound was demonstrated in the start of the letter's name.

It represents the combination of calmness and activity in equal proportions.

It represents it is a reminder that during times of change, it is necessary to incorporate in equal proportion the qualities of quietude with activity.

It represents and it is a reminder of the clear and fortunate choices you made in the past and future.

It represents that resting in the chariot of Yahovah, you are ready for activity with staff and flail in your hands.

Change is an opportunity.

There are four animals that are symbolic representations of change:

1.) The bull (real results)
2.) The lion (imagination)
3.) The man (risk and initiate)
4.) The eagle (spirit and meaning)

They all dwell within the wheels of the chariot of Yahovah.

The chariot illustrates that change is pervasive in that it touches each person Multidimensionally.

The four pillars, four wheels, four cherubim, and the ball of gold, all represent the five elements or the elemental aspects of who we are mentally, psychologically, physically, morally, and spiritually.

The charioteer holds the golden wheel of destiny in his hands, reminding us that through choice, we have the ability to select fortunate, positive abundant changes for ourselves.

In times of contemplating changes that we want to make, it is important for us to access which changes will assist our growth and which ones will be supporting to us at this point in time.

Change is an opportunity to expand realities.

When we combine our emotional nature with our mind and life force, we can produce tangible results that have been fired and stimulated by the motivating force of intuition and perception.

Our choices during times of change are ultimately correct and motivate a deeper commitment to the original purpose of personal and transpersonal existence.

In order to come into the fullness of who we are, it is important to balance the apparent paradoxes, oppositions, or polarities within ourselves.

My satisfaction comes by the spoken word of Yahovah.

Yahovah is my fence.

A fence represents devotion to the word of Yahovah.

> You are all I want Yahvah; I promise to obey your
> word. I ask you with all my heart to have mercy

WAKE UP CALL

on me, as you have promised! I have considered my conduct, and I promise to follow your instructions.

Without delay I hurry to obey your commands. The wicked have laid a trap for me, but I don't forget your word.

In the middle of the night I wake up to praise your righteous judgments. I am a friend of all who serve you, of all who obey your word.

Yahvah, the world is full of your constant love; teach me your commandments. (Psalm 119:57-62)

ט ט ט ט ט ט ט ט ט ט ט ט ט ט ט ט ט ט

TE, J'E, F = ט
= (TET, TETH, J'ETH)

ט = *te, j'e* = *tet* = #9 = Leo = ruby

= red = luster = strength

= passion = power = force = lion

= the word = spool = cylinder

= tribe of Judah = wisdom

= Yahvah be praised = scroll

= book = energy = zeal = hook

= the universal principle of strength, zeal, and luster

    It represents there is a beauty in our nature that quells the beast within our body and mind.

    It represents the removal of all masks so you can see the true inner person or self.

    It represents removing the mask in us and others so you can see inside.

    The mask cutter represents the inherent faith within ourselves to do it and complete and the task given to do.

    It represents how to overcome change by using Yahshua's creative power.

    We must be in our joy, radiance, and luster to be in our strength.

    All people who exhibit strength also exhibit an inherent luster or radiance.

    Strength and luster are qualities that are inseparable.

WAKE UP CALL

Through utilizing our creative gifts and talents, we tame the beasts within.

~ the chastening power of the word ~

~ scroll ~ book ~ the word ~

Yahvah will give you insights and ingenious ideas so unusual that every person will know that Yahvah is at work in your life.

It represents the value of the word of Yahvah.

Psalm 119: 65-72

> You have kept your promise, Yahvah, and been good to your servant. Give me wisdom and knowledge, because I trust in your commands.
>
> Before you awakened me I used to go wrong, but now I obey your word.
>
> How good you are-how kind! Teach me your commands.
>
> Proud men have told lies about me, but with all my heart I obey your instructions.
>
> These men have no understanding of your word, but I find pleasure and happiness in your word.
>
> My awakening was good for me, because it made me learn your commands. The word that you gave me means more to me, than all the money in the world.

JAMES GARNER

Y, I = י
= (YOD, YUD, IOTA, JOT)

י = Y, I = *yod* = #10 = Virgo = green

= peridot = the hermit = virgin

= furrow = safety = line = ears

= strengthening = completion

= reinforcement = increase

= fortification = defense

= tribe of Simeon = protection

= one who hears = meditation

= his arm or his hand = shield

= the universal principle of completion, contemplation, and introspection

This letter has always been the tenth letter and first made the *y* sound and later the *i* sound and meant "arm or hand of Yahovah, the wise man, the lantern bearer, the waymaker."

It represents drawing from internal wisdom and life's experiences as a resource to assist others through the process of life.

It represents the watchdog, keeper, or guardian over the underworld and the dead.

It represents making sure things are complete before we move our attention forward.

It represents that in all states of introspection and contemplation, we must find the unknown parts of oneself that are necessary to experience wholeness and/or completion.

It represents the color of blood, which represents the inherent integrity and honesty within each individual.

It represents you are covered by the blood and body of Yahshua.

It represents being committed to and attending to the details of organization and beauty.

It represents the capacity to give birth to new physical and spiritual life forms.

It represents the completion of things tide to the past so you are free to give birth to new life forms.

It is the state of consciousness and completion.

~ the root of the powers of fire, energy, strength, velocity, vigor, and force ~

~ a solar-phallic outburst of flame, power, strength, energy, or force ~

It represents the use of natural forces as opposed to invoked forces of power. As you dwell in the presence of Yahvah, he will heal your mind, soul, and body, and all infirmities will disappear.

We are all in the hand of Yah, his hand, the justice of the word of Yahvah.

> You created me and you keep me safe; give me understanding so that I may learn your word. Those who have reverence for you will be glad when they see me, because I trust in your promise. I know your judgments are righteous, Yahvah, and that you punished me because you are faithful. Let your constant love comfort me, as you have promised me, your servant. Have mercy on me and I will live, because I take pleasure in your word. May the proud be ashamed for falsely accusing me: as for me, be ashamed for falsely accusing me; as for me, I will meditate on your instructions. May those who

have reverence for you to come to me-all those who know your commands. May I perfectly obey your commandments and be spared the shame of defeat. (Psalm 119-73-80)

ככככככככככככככככככככ

K = כ
= (KAF, KAPH, QOPH, KAPPA)

כ = K = *kaph* = #11 = Jupiter

= circle of destiny = kismet

= the wheel of fortune

= chance = breakthrough

= prosperity = abundance

= opportunity = wealth

= prospect = divine control

= a pan = palm of hand

= spiritual power = flexible

= the universal principle of opportunity, advancement, prosperity, and expansion

The letter *k* is the eleventh letter and has always made the [k] sound with a *k* or *q* means "the three fingers of the palm of the hand of Yahovah."

In scientific and mathematical terminology, the letter *k* means something tenth in sequence, since it is the tenth letter of the Greek alphabet copied from the Phoenician or Shemite alphabet.

It is the last letter of the mathematical equation of phi-beta-kappa, meaning "learn to appreciate the beauty of mathematics."

It represents that Jupiter is the planet of good fortune, opportunity, and abundance.

It represents we can turn our lives in more positive direction by being objective, flexible, and always reaching for new opportunities by turning stars into lightning bolts.

It represents the experience of awakening to the possibilities that will turn around our life in a more positive and expansive direction.

It represents it is a reminder that expansion and abundance come with the willingness to change and keep things moving positively and by taking risks and being open to new opportunities, thinking circular and not linear.

My source of hope is in the palm of his hand, Yahovah.

~ palm of hand ~

A Prayer for Deliverance

> I am worn out, Yahvah waiting for you to save me; I place my trust in your word.
>
> My eyes are tired of watching for what you promised, while I ask, "When will you help me?"
>
> I am as useless as a discarded wineskin; yet I have not forgotten your commands. How much longer must I wait?
>
> When will you punish those who persecute me? Proud people do not obey your word have dug pits to trap me!
>
> Your commandments are all trustworthy; men persecute me with lies-help me!
>
> They have almost succeeded in killing me, but I have not neglected your commands.
>
> Because of your constant love, be good to me, so that I can obey your word. (Psalm 119:81-88)

JAMES GARNER

L = ל
= (LA' MED, LAMBDA)

ל = L, la = *la'med* = #12 = Libra

= sapphire = deep blue = force

= adjustment = justice = drive

= balance = the scales = power

= authority = weight = hero

= tribe of Dan = realignment

= the judge = influence = prod

= ox goad = shepherd's staff

= the universal principle of balance, justice, and realignment

The letter *l* has always been the twelfth letter of the alphabet and made the *l* sound that meant ox goad or a shepherd's *l* shaped herding stick, a short staff that could be hung on the arm and later was adopted by the Greeks.

It reflects all the standards of negotiation and truth.

The letter *l* has been used to represent Yahovah El Shedia and his power to balance the scales.

It represents piercing the web and veil of illusion, delusion, and deception.

Law, truth, justice, and judgment of the living and the dead.

In the scales is the beginning and the end.

It represents whatever is initiated or begun must always be completed at some time.

It represents financial balance.

It represents your formulated ideas and thoughts.

It represents the integrating, balancing, and synthesizing mind, which is often expressed through writing, research, and design.

It represents the application of creative ideas in tangible, useful ways.

It represents the balance of complete health mentally, emotionally, physically, and spiritually.

It represents real touchable ideas to act upon.

It represents that the ultimate guidance for balance comes from within your spirit.

Yah's word will stand for eternity.

Ox goad, shepherd's staff-you will find favor with key people and your level of influence will increase.

It represents faith in the word of Yahovah.

> Your word, Yahvah will last forever, it is eternal in heaven. Your faithfulness endures through all the ages; you have set the earth in place and it remains. All things remain to this day because of your commands, because they are all your servants.
>
> If your word had not been the source of my joy, I would have died from my sufferings. I will never neglect your instructions, because by them you have kept me alive. I am yours-save me!
>
> I have tried to obey your commands. Wicked men are waiting to kill me, but I will meditate on your word.
>
> I have learned that everything has limits; but your commandments are perfect. (Psalm 119-89-96)

WAKE UP CALL

מ מ מ מ מ מ מ מ מ מ מ מ מ מ מ מ

M = מ
= (MEM, MU)

מ = M = *mem* = #13 = water = river

= source of all wisdom = lake

= blue green = waves = ocean

= the hanged man = the guide

= spiritually unconscious

= surrender to Yahovah

= the pattern breaker = yield

= the deep = tidal wave

= love of the word = my source

= the cross over the pyramids

= the universal principle of awakening, surrender, and patter breaking

    The letter *m* has always been placed as the thirteenth letter and made the *m* sound and meant "waves or water."

    It represents the symbol of unlimited life force, constantly available and accessible for creative use.

    It represents that in order to break old patterns, it is necessary to take a different posture or stance to move forward in a new direction for yourself.

    It represents that you must turn it around or even upside down in order to get yourself out of a stuck place and move forward and/or to complete the task given.

It represents nothing is renewed when we are fixated or stuck in the past, present, or future.

It represents to reverse your perception and to surrender to Yahovah.

There are always many more options, solutions, and perspectives to consider than those I am currently invested in.

Asking for help or giving help to others in need.

It represents hang-ups can either prevent our growth or serve as our guide to growth, so the solution is found in our willingness to surrender to a greater sense of faith and trust in a higher source, Yahovah.

It represents you have awakened to and have recognized limiting patterns in your life that need to be broken and/or changed to move ahead.

It represents a time to surrender and move beyond our self-image and needs in order to trust the deeper spiritual wisdom within our spirit being that must be expressed daily.

When we release our limiting destructive patterns, we are freed to openly express our inherent love with wisdom in the world.

Water is the universal symbol for the unconscious mind. Water symbolizes a human's spirituality; spirituality does not necessarily refer to a religious doctrine, but rather to how closely the human lives according to Yahovah's word, not legalism.

It shows us we must love ourselves enough to break bad destructive patters within our personality.

~ the root of the powers of water, fertility, productiveness, beauty, pleasure, and happiness ~

It represents the word of Yahovah is the source of all wisdom ~

~ wave ~ water ~

~ as are the waves of the sea ~

It represents love for the word of Yahvah.

How I love your word! I think about it all day long. Your commandments are with me at all times and it makes me wiser than my enemies. I understand more than all my teachers, because I meditate on your instructions. I have greater wisdom than old men, because I obey your words.

I have avoided all evil conduct, because I want to obey your word. I have not neglected your instructions, because you yourself are my teacher. How sweet are the taste of your instructions- sweeter even than honey! I gain wisdom from your word, so I detest all bad conduct. (Psalm 119:97-104)

נננ

N = נ
= (NUN, NU)

נ = N = *nun* = #14 = Scorpio = peace

= scorpion = topaz = yellow

= birth = death = rebirth

= reborn = moving forward

= release = detachment = bones

= illumination = revival

= my light is the word of Yah

= tribe of Issachar = cobra

= fish swimming = snake

= snake moving forward

= my reward will come

= the universal principle of letting go and moving forward

The letter *n* has always been the fourteenth letter of the alphabet and made the *n* sound. It symbolizes a snake and/or fish and has symbolized all the words above.

It represents that only through letting go are we able to give birth to new life forms. There are three types of transformation in our life span:

1.) To protect and take care of yourself
2.) Letting go of the old so we can make new life experiences

3.) The wisdom and perspective that is needed to become more of who we are meant to be and what we are preordained to do in life.

The skeleton is the inherent structure within our body that holds us up, allows us to arise, move, and go forward, and was never designed to move backward.

The sickle allows you to harvest what you and your brothers have sown at the right time.

It represents as a son of Yahovah. You wear the crown of a king.

It represents the dry bones of who we are.

It represents our ancestral lineage of repeated experiences.

It represents "the crown of the phoenix," an expanded consciousness with Yahovah. It also is to remind us that death, itself, is a rebirth experience.

It represents and is the ability to cut through things and problems for the purpose of a greater harvest.

It represents that by letting go we are able to allow new life to emerge.

It represents that Yahovah's word is the source of all light, a fish (you) swimming in the light.

Though you have endured stress, heartache, and anxiety, Yahvah will fill your life and home with peace.

It represents the capacity to cut through things for the purpose of a greater harvest.

It represents light from the word of Yahvah.

> Your word is a lamp to guide me and a light for my pathway. I will keep my solemn promise to obey your just instructions. My sufferings, Yahovah, were terrible indeed: keep me alive as you have promised. Accept my prayers of thanks, O Yahovah, and teach me your ways.
>
> I am always ready to risk my life; I have not forgotten your word. Wicked men lay a trap for me, but I have not disobeyed your commands.

Your commandments are my eternal possession; they are the joy of my heart. I have decided to obey your word until the day I die. (Psalm 119:104-112)

ססססססססססססססססס

S = ס
= (SAMEKH, SA'MECH)

ס = S = *sa'mech* = #15 = Sagittarius
= blue zircon / jasper = opal
= all colors = synergy = art
= synthesis = mathematics
= safety in the word of Yah
= fusion of the elements = mix
= a prop or stand / to hold up
= tribe of Naphtali = science
= red and white = temperance
= my wresting = deliverance
= pillar = the archer = bow
= the universal principle of synergy, synthesis, and integration

The fifteenth letter, *s*, in the Hebrew alphabet means "prop or pillar."

It represents the union of the oppositions, which creates something new. It represents the combining of the elements to make one greater ingredient. It represents that in order to come into the fullness of who we are, it is important to balance the apparent paradoxes, oppositions, and/or polarities within oneself.

Real synergy is the union of two or more principles, which, when combined, can create a greater opening. It represents the light and dark parts of our nature that need to be incorporated together before we can fully express who we are. Equal parts of lightness and darkness combined make a more balanced and tempered person.

The four distinct facets of the human are his physical, mental, spiritual, and emotional sides.

The precise meaning of a specific element can be determined or illuminated by the conditions and colors of the vision or dream or elements given.

All details must be intertwined in order to arrive at the correct implication of the elements. The support of our hope is in the chosen word, a prop to hold up, a prop or stand to mix in, a metal prop or support.

Yahvah will deliver you from all the things you have wrestled with in your mind, body, and spirit.

It represents that safety is in the word of Yahvah, who is Yahshua.

> I detest those who are not completely loyal to you, but I love your word. You are my defender and protector. I put my hope in your promise. Go away from me and you people that want to commit sin; I will obey the commands of my Yah. Give me strength as you have promised and I shall live; don't let me be disappointed in my hope! Hold me, Yahvah, and I will be safe, and I will always pay attention to your commands. You reject everyone who disobeys your word; either deceitful schemes are useless. You will treat all the wicked like rubbish, and so I love your instructions. Because of you I am not afraid; I am filled with praise because of your judgments. (Psalm 119:113-120)

_____
_____
_____
_____
_____
_____
_____
_____

U, O =
= ('AYIN, AIN, MICRON)

- = U = *ain* = #16 = Capricorn = goat
- = garnet = burgundy = healing
- = procreation = blood = rest
- = transformation = sex = wit
- = spirit = vision = comedy
- = tribe of Zebulon = the eyes
- = glorious dwelling place
- = home of rest = watch = look
- = the little *o* = fountain
- = the universal principle of laughter and humor and looking at what is transforming us

The letter *o* has been the sixteenth letter and symbolized eyes since Egyptian slaves reformed the Adamic alphabet in about 2000 BC.

This is the only letter that has gone through a transformation within itself. (During the Middle Ages, this letter or symbol was changed from the goat and cross of Moses to the devil by religious leaders that did not know the meaning of the letter or the meaning of complete healing, and thus the word *devil* was created by misguided religious leaders that wanted to enslave the public. When spelled backward, it says *lived*, or should I say once lived to try to quell paganistic cults of tree worship and animal worship.) This is what started the backward teaching of religious Christians and Satanic cults that still exist today. This was supposed to make way for the new false belief system manifested by the Catholic Church doctrines.

The symbol means that we need to face the problems at hand and not disguise them in religious party dogmas of men, not Yahovah. This letter stands for the fact that there is happiness when walking with Yahvah.

We are not visiting the morgue. We are visiting Yahovah; therefore, you should be happy and merry because you have been redeemed by Yahshua.

It represents that we must face whatever is against us with tenacity and humor together ¬

It represents that we can face and move through the spiderweb, sure-footed and with humor, for Hasatan has none of these attributes because the cross of Yahshua stands over his grave.

This symbol reminds us that if we take our problems too seriously, they can and will ensnare us and take us off balance. This symbol represents the need to hold on to both the qualities of mirth, stability, and centeredness in facing real or self-imagined problems that throw us off balance.

The word of Yahvah is my source of confidence. It represents the eye of Yahvah. It represents that only Yahvah will fill you with a double portion of his power. It represents obedience of the word of Yah.

> I have done what is right and good; don't abandon me to my enemies. You promise that you will help your servant; don't let arrogant men oppress me! My eyes are tired from watching for your saving help, for the deliverance you have promised.
>
> Treat me according to your constant love, and teach me your commands. I am your servant; give me understanding, so that I will know your teachings.
>
> Yahovah, it is time for you to act, because people are disobeying your word. I love your commands more than gold, more than the finest gold. And so

JAMES GARNER

I will follow your instructions; I detest all wrong ways. (Psalm 119:121-128)

פפפפפפפפפפפפפפפפפפפפ

P = פ
= (PEH, PE, PAY, PI, PIE, PEE)

פ = P = peh = #17 = Mars = tower
= red-orange = modernization
= demolition = construction
= renovation = reformation
= reinstatement = curing
= restructuring = spoken
= the power of healing
= the mouth = healing = speak
= circumference to diameter
= the universal principle of repair, restoration, and renovation through speech, the spoken word.

The letter *p* was the seventeenth letter and is now the sixteenth letter and has always made the *p* sound.

It symbolizes the aspect of the mouth and all the words above.

Originally Semitic then taken by the Greeks as with all Greek letters, the letter *p* itself meant nothing unlike the alphabets they copied the letter from.

Today, pi represents the most famous ratio in mathematics, namely, that of a circle's circumference to its diameter, the number of times the circle would sit atop its circumference. This ratio is approximated at 3.14, but in fact it is an irrational number that begins as 3.1415926535 and actually really mathematically calculates to the equation of infinity.

It represents the reorganization of old forms into new life forms. It represents the transformation and awakening required to make the right changes in life on earth. It represents the spiritual life force within us that requires that we dismantle all our habits and restructure them in a more natural order that walks with Christ.

It represents that in order to move forward, you must dismantle and remove that which is artificial, false to fact, and no longer a part of the authentic or essential inner self so we can walk in the right pathway of Yahovah.

It is a state of awakening to the deeper aspects and genuine aspects of ourselves and the point of life. Once we awaken, we are required to come into alignment with who we are in Christ Yahshua.

It represents Yahovah's process of restructuring in order to heal, renovate, and restore the whole inner self, mind, and body completely.

It represents there is an inner peace that comes only when we return to Christ the characteristics of who we actually are spiritually.

It represents the essential and genuine aspects of who you really are, fully restored only in Christ Yahshua.

It represents the removing of old ways or traditions of men in order to manifest Yahovah's power from heaven onto his earth.

The tower is the external manifestation of the internal chariot that Yahovah has positioned within is.

My guidance comes by the spoken word of Yahovah, the mouth.

It represents the desire to obey the word of Yahovah.

> Your teachings are wonderful; I obey them with all my heart. The explanation of your teachings gives light and brings wisdom to the ignorant. In my desire for your commands I pant with an open mouth. Turn to me and have mercy on me as you do all those who love you. As you have promised keep me from falling; don't let me be overcome by evil. Save me from those who oppress me, so that I may obey your commands. Bless me with your presence and teach me your laws. My tears

WAKE UP CALL

pour down like a river, because people do not obey your word. (Psalm 119:129-136)

TZ, TS, X = צ
= (TZADEH, TZAD'DI, TSADE)

צ = TS = *tzadeh* = #18 = Saturn
= Aries = diamond = fire = clear
= red, orange, yellow, green
= purple, blue = a sickle = ram
= fleur-de-lis = the emperor
= rule = leadership = control
= tribe of Gad = relationship
= troublesome fortune
= the universal principle of power and leadership

The letter *ts* is the eighteenth letter of the Hebrew alphabet and means "fire" or one of the corresponding words above.

It represents the pioneer, the builder, the leader, the doer, the visionary, the traveler.

It represents one who has the ability to make things stable, solid, and secure for himself and others.

It represents adventure and exploration.

It represents the total color of fire.

It represents the symbol of nature's source of all light.

It reminds us that all leadership requires vision and forethought.

It represents that if you don't have clear vision, you can't lead into the future; you lead into the past.

The fleur-de-lis of fire (the union of mind, heart, and spirit), the three-pronged flame ~

It represents yang energy, or masculine energy.

It represents being strong but sensitive.

It represents that leadership is a quality that is constantly changing both internally and externally in our lives.

It reminds us that all effective leadership requires union of heart, mind, and spirit in making good decisions and taking action on the right plans.

The emperor represents the kind of leadership that is strong enough to make war yet sensitive to negotiation and peacemaking.

The double phoenix-it represents the word is my prayer for blessing.

Relationships that have brought you heartache will be restored.

It represents the character of the word of Yah.

It represents the sickle of the word that cuts out, cut out.

It represents the justice of the word of Yahvah.

You are righteous, Yahvah, your words are just. The rules that you have given are completely fair and just. My anger burns in me like fire, because my enemies disregard your commands. How certain your promise is! How I love it! I am unimportant and despised, but I do not neglect your teachings. Your righteousness will last forever, and your word is always true. I am filled with trouble and anxiety, but your commandments bring me joy. Your instructions are always just; give me understanding, and I will live (Psalm 119:137-144)

קקקקקקקקקקקקקקקקק

Q, QU = ק
= (QOPH, KOPH, KAPH, QOPPA, QU) =

ק = Q = *kuf* = # 19 = Pisces = Ape =
= the moon = the gates = way in
= aquamarine = opal = access =
= the door = joy = entrance =
= sight and balance control =
= source of strength = head =
= tribe of Asher = happiness =
= back of the head or brain =
Cerebellum = reading images =

   The universal principle of choice - making, authenticity and access ~
   ~ The letter "Q" is the nineteenth letter of the Hebrew alphabet and meant the back of the human head or an ape
   ~ It represents the process of choosing our authentic expression or our false dutiful expression ~
   ~ It represents that we must let go of the old in order to go threw the gates and experience anything new ~
   ~ It represents the choice to be genuine or false ~
   ~ It represents that every day we are at the gates to make the choice to leave old patterns of enslavement to the known world or moving threw the gates of heaven to explore the unknown real world ~
   ~ Choice has three functions ~

WAKE UP CALL

~ By choice we create new realities or sustain and maintain current realities or release and let go of realities that no longer serve us ~

~ The gates symbolize the renewal of life and the reality of eternal existence ~

~ It represents the moons magnetic powers upon the water of the earth reminding us that the inbuilt power of our receptive personality is to open, expand, yield and totally communicate our full power, potential and personality as the moon ~

~ As with any fable the moon can bring inspiration or illusion and deception ¬

~ It represents the word of Yah is my source of strength ~

~ The back of the head ~

~ The back of the brain ~

~ Yahvah will fill your life with unprecedented joy and happiness ~

~ A prayer for deliverance ~

~ Ps. 119; 145-152 ~

~ With all my heart I call to you, Yahvah and I will obey your commands!

I call to you, save me and I will keep your word.

Before sunrise I call to you for help; I place my hope in your promise.

All night long I lie awake, to meditate on your instructions.

Because your love is constant hear me, O Yahvah; show me your mercy and preserve my life!

My cruel persecutors are coming closer, people who never keep your law.

But you are near to me, Yahvah, and all your commands are permanent. Long ago I learned about your instructions; you made them to last forever! (Psalm 119:137-152)

_____
_____
_____
_____
_____
_____
_____

ררררררררררררררררר

R = ר

= (RESH, RHO)

ר = R = *resh* = #20 = RAINBOW =
= the sun = teamwork = promise
= partnership = alliance = son
= the brains cerebrum =
= intelligence = memory = head
= divine motivation = ideas =
= dreams = visions = translate
= inspiration = brainwaves =
= the front of your head =
= thoughts = consciousness =

The universal principle of teamwork, partnership, and cooperation ~
~ The letter "R" was the twentieth letter of the Hebrew alphabet and made the "R" sound and meant the whole head ~
~ The sun depicts the unlimited life force that is within us waiting to be used and expressed by oneself ~
~ It is the divine child in all of us always seeking in unlimited ways ~

It represents inspiration and joy coming into practical and useable form.

It represents the unlimited reservoir of creativity inside.

It represents the inner dance of inventiveness within all of us.

The sun reveals we are natural generators, motivators, and stimulators, so we can bring unity to our relationships.

It represents that teamwork is a transformative experience, which requires trust in spiritual and physical processes working simultaneously together to create a group or team.

It represents that teamwork and partnership are often for the purpose of implementing shared creative vision.

It represents that all creative processes are a form of play and exploration.

It represents that our basic natures unfold and revitalize with every inspired practice and implementation of our expression.

It represents the joy and excitement of inspiration.

It represents joy and inspiration coming into practical and useable form.

It represents the word of Yahvah is my source of deliverance.

~ the front of your head ~
~ the front of your brain ~
~ brainwaves ~

> Look at my suffering and save me, because I have not neglected your word. Defend my cause and set me free; as you have promised. The wicked will not be saved, for they do not obey your word. But your compassion is great; show your mercy and save me!
>
> I have many enemies and oppressors, but I do not fail to obey your word. When I look at those traitors, I am filled with disgust, because they do not keep your commands.

See how I love your instructions, Yahvah. Your love never changes, save me!

The heart of your word is truth, and all your righteous judgments are eternal. (Psalm 119:153-160)

SH, SCH, C = שׁ
= (SHIN, SCHIN, SIGMA)

שׁ = C = shin = #21 = fire = insight

= the *aeon* = discernment = Yah

= tooth or teeth = prophecy

= source of peace = work

= good judgment = family

= ancestor = sensitivity

= revelation = visualization

= profession = inspired vision

= the angel or the messenger

= blowing the trumpet

= the last judgment

= human emotions

= the universal principle of good judgment and discernment

The letter *sh* is the twenty-first letter of the Hebrew alphabet and means "tooth or teeth" and the words above.

The Hebrew *schin* takes the *sh* sound and, unlike most Hebrew letters, still resembles its Phoenician forbearer in shape.

It represents good judgment in personal and specialized situations.

It represents a state of an indefinite period of time and space.

It reminds us of our creative power to give birth to new life forms and ideas from our insight.

It is our creative and specialized power to create new ideas from inspired vision.

It represents that all perceptions come from our ability to take a look from the whole perspective to gain insight on the right direction to take and go in correctly for the right results.

~ inspired vision ~

It reflects that wisdom comes from experience and is not randomly spoken or given.

It represents creative and professional power at all levels.

It represents that properly used creativity benefits all.

It represents integration of all personal and professional aspects of our lives.

It reminds us of our inherent power to create and give birth to new ideas or dreams, when we talk with Yahovah and listen to his voice.

The perception of Yahovah is needed as we give birth to new ideas in both family and career.

The *aeon* reminds us to look at our history and forgive ourselves and others for the judgments we are making about what we are doing or not doing in our lives.

Fire is a complex symbol. It can symbolize passion, anger, the spirit, cooking, purification, transformation, illumination, and destruction. Just as fire burns, so, too, it symbolizes our burning emotions, those that are fed by the fuels of obsessions that are not from Yah.

Fire symbolizes the extreme and dangerous intensity of human emotions.

The messenger or angel of the Lord that blows the trumpet that raises the dead.

The word of Yah is my source of all peace.

~ teeth ~

It represents my dedication to the word of Yahvah.

> Powerful men attack me unjustly, but I respect your word. How happy I am because of your

promises-as happy as someone who has found a rich treasure.

I hate and detest all lies, but I love your word. Seven times each day I thank you for your righteous judgments.

Those who love your word have perfect security, and there is nothing that can make them fall.

I wait for you to save me and I wait for your commands. I obey your teaching; I love them with all my heart, I obey your commands and instructions; you see everything I do. (Psalm 119:162-168)

JAMES GARNER

תתתתתתתתתתתתתתתתת

TA, T = ת
= (TAV, TAU, TAW)

ת = T = *tav* = #22 = completeness
= all of the elements = Saturn
= earth = unity = combination
= the universe = the big *O*
= harmonization = complete
= totality = creation = essence
= my heart's signature = union
= the heart = your signature
= the sign of the cross = *x* on *o*
= the sign of extension
= omega = truth

It is the universal principle of individualization, totality, and unity.

The letter *t* is the last letter of the Phoenician and the Hebrew alphabet, letter 22, and took the *t* sound that began its name and meant "the mark signature" or one of the words above.

So then, even though *t* is the twenty-second letter of the alphabet, so it becomes twenty-one, and the letter *a* becomes zero when legalized into religious law by Jewish leaders.

It represents that in order to become free and more individuated, it is important to simultaneously let go and move forward. The universe represents the ability to be at home in the external world and the internal world within us.

So with the sword of the spoken word, I cut through the limitations and restrictions of life and I weave them into a net to dance and sing on.

It symbolizes the unity of positive and negative forces both internally and externally.

The number 213 represents all the fives elements of earth, fire, water, air, and spirit.

It represents returning back to the original vision of Yahovah.

It is a symbol of the ability to be balanced in the expression of being equally vibrant and compelling simultaneously.

It represents the completion and integration of a great inner work that has involved the unifying of polarities, oppositions, and paradoxes within oneself and humanity.

It symbolizes you must simultaneously let go to move forward.

It represents that you are required to transform before you can experience new worlds externally and internally.

It represents that change requires that we grow from our mistakes to expand our awareness.

It represents the ability to be at home wherever you are.

The five elements are the following:

1. Earth - Taurus, the bull
2. Fire - Leo, the lion
3. Water - Scorpio, the eagle
4. Air - Aquarius, the man
5. Spirit - the eye of Yahovah

It represents that it is important to express ourselves completely - physically (the bull), creatively (the lion), emotionally (the eagle), mentally (the man), spiritually (the eye).

The animals represent what it is like to be in or out of our elements.

Tau means "the sign of the cross or the sign of extension."

The letters *a* and *t* together mean the beginning and the end of the essence of extension.

The earth is a symbol of a human's physical aspect. It represents that it is the earth we were made from. On earth we physically encounter life's issues and obstacles.

The earth can indicate the direction of the physical body; it can reveal whether the person is remaining stationary or retreating to safe and easy paths or the condition of the human's physical path.

It represents the root of the powers of the earth, material gain, power, labor, wealth, and contentment.'

The affirmation of the identity of the sun and earth, spirit and flesh.

Your word is a prayer of blessing.

Your signature of giving your heart to the word.

Your heart.

Yahvah has heard the cries of your heart and placed a hedge of protection all around you.

> Let my cry for help reach you, Yahvah. Give me understanding as you have promised. Listen to my prayers and save me according to your promises.
>
> I will always praise you, because you teach me your word. I will sing about your word, because your commands are just. Always be ready to help me because I follow your commands, your voice.
>
> How I long for your saving help, O Yahvah!
>
> I find happiness in your word, give me life so that I may praise you; your instructions will help me.
>
> I wander about like a lost sheep; so come look for me, your servant, because, I have not neglected your word! (Psalm 119:169-176)

WOE TO THOSE WHO DO NOT TAKE HEED TO MY WORD, THE SPIRIT OF TRUTH

דִרוּ יָם תֹ ת דְרָה תֹ הוּ דֹ תְנַ כֵּ־ת דְרָה תֹ סֵהֹת תֹ וֶ
הִתְרַת הֵת ט תִרְפָּס הֵת:

1. Woe to those who do not repent daily.
2. Woe to those who have haughty eyes that always look to condemn.
3. Woe to those who lie and act as if they do not know that I know they lie with every breath.
4. Woe to those who always try to hurt those that are innocent and blame the not guilty.
5. Woe to those who shed the blood of those who are innocent and unable to protect themselves.
6. Woe to those who wish to hold evil schemes in their hearts always to hurt others or me.
7. Woe to those who are always out to do evil things to my creation and my people.
8. Woe to those who bear a false witness against their brother and lie with their every breath.

9. Woe to those bear a false witness of testimony and my word.
10. Woe to those who are always trying to cause strife among his brothers and his nation.
11. Woe to those who make idols an image to worship other than Yahovah, which is an abomination to the Lord.
12. Woe to those who try to dishonor their father or their mother.
13. Woe to those who move their neighbors' boundary markers.
14. Woe to those who mislead lost or blind people and cause them harm.
15. Woe to those who distort the justice due anyone.
16. Woe to those who have sex with their father's wife, because he has uncovered his father's skirt.
17. Woe to those who have sex with any animal or someone of the opposite sex.
18. Woe to those who have sex with their sister or brother, the son or daughter of his or her father and mother.
19. Woe to those who have sex with his or her father- or mother-in-law.
20. Woe to those who try to harm their neighbor in secret.
21. Woe to those who accept a bribe against an innocent person.
22. Woe to those who do not confirm my words of the truth by doing them.
23. Woe to those hypocrites that waste their time on religion instead of a relationship with Yahovah.
24. Woe to those who walk away from my son's living word.
25. Woe to those scribes and Pharisees, hypocrites, because you have shut off the kingdom of heaven from men; for you do not enter in yourselves nor do you allow those who are entering to go in.
26. Woe to those scribes and Pharisees, hypocrites. Because you seek to devour widows' houses, even while for a pretense you make long prayers; therefore, you will receive greater condemnation.
27. Woe to those scribes and Pharisees, hypocrites, because you travel about on sea and land to make one new proselyte, and when he becomes one, you make him twice a son of hell as yourselves.

28. Woe to you, blind guides who say whoever swears by the temple, that is nothing; but he who swears by the gold in the temple, he is obligated. "You fools and blind men, which is more important, the gold or the temple that sanctified the gold?" And whoever swears by the altar, that is nothing, but whoever swears by the offering upon it, he is obligated by the offering. "You blind men, which is more important, the offering or the altar that sanctifies the offering?" Therefore, he who swears by the altar swears both by the altar and everything on it. "And he that swears by the temple swears both by the temple and him that dwells within it." And he that swears by heaven swears both by the throne of Yah and by him that sits upon it.
29. Woe to those scribes and Pharisees, hypocrites, for you tithe mint and dill and cumin and have neglected the weightier provisions of the law: justice, mercy, and faithfulness; but these are what you should have done without neglecting the others. "You blind guides, you strain out a gnat and swallow a camel!"
30. Woe to you scribes and Pharisees, hypocrites! For you clean the outside of the cup and of the dish, but inside they are full of robbery and self indulgence." You blind Pharisees, first clean the inside of the cup and of the dish, so that the outside of it may become clean also.
31. #31 woe to you scribes and Pharisees, hypocrites! For you are like white-washed tombs that on the outside appear beautiful, but inside they are full of dead bones and all impurity. "Even so you appear righteous to men, but inwardly you are full of hypocrisy and iniquity."
32. Woe to you scribes and Pharisees, hypocrites! For you build tombs, the tombs for dead prophets, and adorn the graves of the righteous and say, "If we had been living in those days of our fathers we would not have become partners with them in shedding the blood of the prophets." Consequently you bear witness against yourselves, that you are sons of those that murdered the prophets. Fill up then the measure of the guilt of your fathers, you serpents, you brood of pit vipers, how shall you escape the sentence of hell?

Therefore, behold, I am sending you prophets and wise men and scribes; some of them you will kill and crucify, and some of them you will scourge in your synagogues and persecute from city to city, that upon you would fall the guilt of all the righteous bloodshed on the earth, from the blood of righteous Abel unto the blood of Zechariah, the son of Berechiah, whom you murdered between the temple and the altar. Truly I say to you, all these things will come upon this generation.

THE SEVEN ABOMINATIONS (PROVERBS 6:16-19)

These are six things which the Lord hates, yes, seven which are an abomination to him:

1. Haughty eyes
2. A lying tongue
3. Hands that shed innocent blood
4. A heart that devises wicked plans
5. Feet that run rapidly to evil
6. A false witness who utters lies
7. One who spreads strife among brothers

THE TWELVE CURSES OF MOUNT EBAL (DEUTERONOMY 27:15-16)

1. Cursed is the man who makes an idol, a molten image, an abomination to the Lord, the work of the hands of the craftsman.
2. Cursed is the man that dishonors their father or their mother.
3. Cursed is he that moves his neighbor's boundary mark.

4. Cursed is he that misleads a lost blind person on the road.
5. Cursed is he that distorts justice due anyone.
6. Cursed is he that lies with his father's wife, because he has uncovered his father's skirt.
7. Cursed is he that lies with any animal.
8. Cursed is he that lies with his sister, the daughter of his father or mother.
9. Cursed is he that lies with his mother-in-law.
10. Cursed is he that strikes his neighbor in secret.
11. Cursed is he that accepts a bribe against an innocent person.
12. Cursed is he who does not confirm the words of the law by doing them.

> Also let none of you devise evil in your heart against another, and do not love perjury; for all these are what I hate declares the Lord of hosts. (Zechariah 8:17)

YOU WILL COME FALLING DOWN
נוּדֿ גנִלל־ט מֵשׁ לִלוּ ֹי

Woe to you, all of you who follow Lucifer, you will come falling down with a mighty crash. Even a son cannot go against the father of all things and live. All the armies of heaven await the final word to be spoken. All the fallen angels of the heavens will come crawling back to Yahovah for his forgiveness. He may have mercy for now on those that wish redemption, but soon all chances for redemption will be over for the living and the dead.

Woe to you Satan, all your unholy spirits, you wimpy angels, you false prophets, and your fake son. I saw you all come falling down with a mighty crash and lose your inheritance forever, because of your ignorance, arrogance, pridefulness, and deceitfulness against Yahovah, his teachings, and his ways.

Woe to you, Pharaoh, your false priests, your feral spirits, and false gods. There is but on living Yah, and you are not him, nor will you ever be like him. You were given a chance to do it the easy way or the hard way. To your own regret, you chose the latter. You shall never set yourself up as a yah nor go against him. You cannot stand in the face of Yahovah; he will consume you. There is but one Yah, and you cannot worship any other.

Woe to you, Baal, Asteroth, and all other pagan idols. There is but one living yah, and you are not him. You are a useless tombstone under a tree reserved only for all the dead gods men worshipped throughout time. You were dead and useless then as you are dead and useless now, as it is written you were and were always dead forever, never to return, for you have been chained to burn in Sheol forever for impersonating a yah.

Woe to you, Babylon, your beast, your false prophet, and your unholy spirit. Babylon the Great has come falling down with a mighty crash. You cannot raise the dead. Only I, Yahovah, can do that. It is written. It will never rise again; it is fallen forever. It is fallen forever in all the heavens, never to be rebuilt.

Woe to you, Jezebel and Ahab, the false king and queen, and all 450 of your false prophets and your foul spirits. You came from the pit of Sheol, and to the fires of hell you were sent years ago, never to return anywhere forever. The hounds of heaven will eat your flesh, lap your blood and torment your souls forever. You cannot stand in the way of a prophet of Yahovah. The fires of heaven will consume you. You cannot go against the living word of Yah.

Woe to you Herod, your false queen, and your ugly little princess. You have been judged guilty of killing my little ones to try to kill me. You were guided by lies from the pit of Sheol, so worms will eat your flesh forever. Somehow you thought you could shut my baptist up, but now his voice is even louder, loud and clear forever: "Make straight the way of the Lord Yahshua. He will come again to judge the quick and the dead."

Woe to you Pharisees, Sadducees, scribes, and false Torah teachers of false laws, builders of the great fake Jewish temple. I, the great I Am, never prescribed you to build or practice your rituals in order to appease me. You have kindled my anger by making my word a show and a Greek temple spectacle mingled with my word to milk the poor of their money in order to make yourselves to be worshipped and rich with no regard for the people you were supposed to be serving. These practices only appease religious men, not Yahovah. No one can go against the living word and survive my wrath or judgements. I am the living word, not the written word. It is to their shame they were unable to see the Messiah even though he was staring them back in the face. Now they will always see Yahshua's face staring back at them with unquenchable fire in his eyes. They lost their inheritance because they were so religious they could not see him, and so religion because, they were so religious they could not see him, and so religion and greed consumed them forever, and they have lost their lives forever to burn in the fires of God's wrath, for their stolen offering I will not accept. They make me sick.

WAKE UP CALL

Woe to you, Caesar, your false priestesses, false gods, and fake temples. I, Yahovah, made you tear down the phony temple you built on my mountain above my ark. There is but one living Yah, and you are not him. You all have come falling down with a mighty crash, never to return again forever. How dare you, for your sheer ignorance, to think you could go against the Lord of all the heavens and live. All the armies of the heavens work for Yahovah, and he decides whom his generals will be. All of you will burn in the fires of heaven. They will consume all of you, and your spirits will exist no more forever and ever, forever.

Woe to you, Islam, your false imams, fake camel-driving illiterate prophet Mohammed, a powerless messiah who came from man and not Yah. You have angered the Lord the most for your treachery against your own brothers. I, the Lord Yahovah, have never sent an illiterate man to do anything without knowing the living word. You have distorted Judaism, which is a distortion in itself. You are and have been worshipping a curse on your own brothers. You found some scrolls in a cave and made up a religion and made yourself a false messiah so that you could have every man's wives. You supposedly floated away, but somehow they can worship your bones. It is written, "No man comes from me whose bones can be worshipped." You died on 666, never to return on the earth, forever chained in Sheol to burn forever, and the orgy you thought you were going to have will be the angels of heaven tormenting your misbegotten souls forever. I will search you all out and take you out one at a time till you all exist no more forever for the killing of the innocent in my name. I will come quickly upon you, and you will not see me coming. Your false messiah died 1,345 years ago and will never live on earth or in heaven again or even come back to visit, because he was a fake messiah then as he is a bigger fake messiah now. You have mocked the Lord thy yah for far too long with your wishes to destroy my kingdom to come, and now your time of doom has come upon you swiftly.

Woe to you, spirits of religion. You have been allowed to exist for far too long, and now your day of reckoning has come. You will come falling down and exist no more forever. My kingdom will come on earth as it is in heaven, and it will be transformed forever.

JWG 10/20/11

VIRUS/ שָׂרִס

Hello, when I contact you, the living word I speak from the mighty Yahvah forms into existence. You have just been infected with the born-again virus. No antivirus can stop it, for it is spiritual. There is now nothing you can do to stop it, so you must read on now or you will surely die. You will never be the same. Once this was written down and was read by you and wired onto the phone system waves and Internet system waves and the digital system waves, it has and it will permeate every part of the earth's system and every part of your mind, body, soul, and spirit in three days.

This virus eats up all evil within it, and it infects the whole earth with the mighty word of Yahvah and is the revenge of Yahvah and his servant Dodo. You are not subject to the laws of the earth anymore. You are a disciple of Yahshua and nothing else. You are born again and are now being turned into a spirit being that is nonreligious and must tell the truth always. This virus is on a mission from Yahvah and was chosen because it is unstoppable and sent by Yahvah. It is a spiritual virus, not a physical virus, and it has no cure. It is on a mission from Yahvah, and now so are you. Uh oh, you thought you were saved, so did I. You gave me your heart, and now I take over. It takes your heart, child of Yah, and I replace it with mine.

All truth and healing go through three steps: first, ridiculed by body and mind, then violently opposed by both, and then all things must be accepted as it is self-evident as the truth to all things. You have now entered a new dimension of time and space. You are in the new life zone. Sorry, no more excuses for you to use or yeah-buts. There are no more roadblocks now, only a clear and open pathway with clear direction on how to enter guiltlessly as a servant of Yahshua, a wide-open door to enter my dining room.

There will be nothing that anyone can do to stop it, for you now know you're infected, and now all the tools you will need are laid out on my banquet table for you to use diligently. You must enter and eat or you will die. Come, my child, and have a seat and sit with me for a while. I want to put the little boy back in you that dreamed big dreams like I do. The dreams that I, Yahvah, gave them only to do. Come sit and rest in my arms awhile so I can look at you and fit you properly with all the garments that you will need for you to complete the job properly and in order. Oh, wow, the enemy can see your holy crown now and must flee from your presence or die. You are now on a mission from Yahvah. A real mission from God! Act like it! Now when you pray in tongues, it will infect your mind and the whole earth with my glory and presence, the living word of the mighty Yahvah.

One man can do it, but it would be better if all my captains work together and in unity of spirits to achieve a greater kingdom.

My child, don't think you are. You must know you are. Let all of your old religious mind-sets go - fear, doubt, disbelief - free your mind of it. Round-file it and leave it in the trash bin.

It is written, "I Yahvah will send you a double portion that would be greater than the former ones. But I have decided to send a triple portion instead so that none could say they did not hear it or know of it and to convene a just court, for there will be no appeals in this court, and all decisions will be just, true, and final. I have sent Moses and Aaron, Dodo and Elisha, Samuel and Gideon, and they all will have the strength of Samson. I have also sent two judges, Yephthah and Samson, two judge, the quick and the dead of all guilt - to redeem and to establish an everlasting kingdom and inheritance.

They will defy the image of the beast. They will trample down all false religious doctrines of priests and priestesses, doctrines of warlocks and witches, evil spirits and demons, principalities and powers of the deep, and angels of the demonic realm. They will come before my son returns to declare his kingdom and reign on earth with him as head, as he already reigns in heaven. They will have legions of mighty heavenly angels from Yahvah to command. They will reign with him on earth and in paradise. They will be unstoppable by any man. They will grow younger, not older, and no sickness will befall them. No poison can hurt them. As a new disciple of the Christ, you are responsible to do the right thing. You will expose a lie or a liar with the truth by exposing the lie. You will find the truth in all things.

You sit across from the enemy of false religion and pagan practices. One wears a beautiful white suit clothed in false pagan religions and false Christian doctrines and pagan practices and false unholy worship of idols, organized cult Christianity. One wears a red suit, and he is clothed with the spirit of Nazism, fascism, socialism, communism, Catholicism, organized cult Christianity, and you are a prisoner of a man and a backwards philosophy that is against all freedoms of the people, murder for profit with the blink of an eye. One wears an all-black suit, the Jew, the worshipper of all evil idols and money and greed. They seek to put the balances in their favor always regardless of any other thing but themselves. One wears a green suit, a follower of Islam, that supposed they would make up a religion and a messiah I never sent so they could eat their own children as a Baal worshipper does and wish to make one to believe they are holy as a Pharisee did, a follower of all earthly desires of the flesh and of the earth and not Yahvah,

They are a follower of the earth and not a steward of it. They all are and have been the followers of all the false religions, and they all will be sent to Sheol instead of heaven. I will burn all their works with holy fire. My seraphim will carry you away forever. They will all find out what suit they all decided to wear and follow instead of my blue suit of the Holy Spirit and my Son, the living word, Yahshua.

Many out of envy will try to stab you in the back, but now that knife will break when they try to use it. Uh, oh, lookout. You have what they will never have through their practices of false religion. Sorry!

It is written: "Many are called but very few are chosen vessels of Yahvah." It is because of what is now in your genes - my body and blood wow! Another new son, a newborn son of mine, I am so proud of you and what you have done and will still do. Your forefathers prayed to be guardians of this day, and now they are your guardian angels from birth from Yahvah. You will all hear the clear unmingled word of Yah, and when they read the scripture, it will be clear and concise with what every other person reads, and all will hear one clear word and nothing different from the clear word of Yahvah. As for those people who wish to continue to lie and twist the truth and play games on my holy word and my holy name, this will be my sign to them. "My children, my name is to be used, not hidden away out of some false witness, their tongues will wither in their very own mouths. They will not be able to speak anymore, and the fake finger they pointed at you will be stuck right back up their very own ass that they decided to ride in on. And with that finger they will wither away as the fig tree. If they point that finger at my sons again, they will receive an eternal and just reward - death forever. I will not look at them with compassion any longer," says Yahvah. "You can lead an ass to living water, but that does not mean that the ass drank from it.

"My children, it is too bad that there are so many prophets of doom and gloom that don't speak my words or even wish to know me but act as if they do at the time of my return, when there should be true fear of Yahvah, true praise, true worship, true dancing and singing, real truth and justice for all, happiness instead of sadness, blessing others instead of cursing them, and not with just those of my family, my color, and my creed, for that is what all lost people do." Arise and shine so your light does not get put out. There is only one way to the Father, that is only through the Son of Yahvah, and his name is Yahshua.

JWG 11/18/11

THE BEGINNING OF THE NEW DAY IT IS HEREBY PROCLAIMED

Welcome to the twenty-first century. Things will change for the better, not the worst. I will do a different thing, says the Lord Yahvah. My child, one day I found you lost and broken in little pieces. I chose you and picked you up and put you on a rock to put you back together again, but then you and the rock I had to put in a furnace, and it drew out all the dross and melted into you and grew into you and you became a fine nugget. It changed your color to mine and transformed you into my image. I put you back together in my image, back together in the image of Yahshua. You are a rainbow of color now with myriads of angels around you. You didn't like the way I was doing it, and you said it didn't look the way you wanted, but, child, I put you back the way I wanted for you to be just like me. I came and revealed myself in and through you.

Those times when you and your loved ones have felt left behind or abandoned are the times when I, the Lord Yah, have come down, stood behind you, and picked you up myself and carried you through the troubles in your lives and put your lives back together. I will never leave you nor forsake you, says the Lord of hosts. Your tests and trials are a test of your quality. How well you pass the test tells me whether you will stand with me or with the world. I have given you all the choice to burn in my holy fire or his eternal burning fire of torture and chains. I have not closed my eyes to the things of today. I have steadfastly looked at today and tomorrow through the eyes of my chosen ones to find a remedy to the troubles of these days.

Woe to you, greedy political racists and supposed Christians, white and black warlocks, as well as little witches. You have judged my ministers of Christ as if I did not know what I was doing and you can somehow fool me. You are the fools, because I have become disgusted with you all unless they plead with me to relent.

Woe to you all, for I have become disgusted with some people that call themselves community action networks, politicians, Christians, and/or pastors, who walk not by the Holy Spirit, but by the spirit of the Antichrist and racism. I call all unto me. I am not color blind,

The new millennium has now begun, and a new age is unfolding, one in which the right kind of change will take place. You have a choice to follow lies and be fooled or follow the truth, which will set you and your country free from the chains that bind us into slavery and loss of all freedoms. *Words are mere words without action.* The truth is always simple. That is why people wish to believe lies instead of the truth, because in believing, they would find the solution is simple, but then they would have to get involved in a more stewardly way to make the right kind of changes to actually solve the problems at hand. In believing, they would have to take action and do something about it as all our forefathers did. They were not more worried about their image than the truth, nor were they color blind. They were fighting for their lives. Honor the forefathers and what they did to build America into the place everyone wants to come to and copy. The right actions will bring about the right passions.

Woe to you, greedy politicians, who walk not in the truth or work or listen to the people till it is too late. Wake up, you can participate in helping to change America, the world, and all of posterity's future. The majority can't keep paying for what one person has done. Deception is not truth; it is a false front meant to lead you on the wrong pathway. You must decide what to do with the time and dream given you. Without action, a dream is just a dream. You must consider all and be a servant of all. You must work for it to come true. You must work on this country to make it better.

"This is my country founded upon my name, and I, the Lord, Yahvah, stand behind it. I will not allow the wrong kind of change in the country founded upon my name and principles. I, the great I Am, dictate the times and seasons, not men. I am against it. I will stop it." Socialism is a stagnant pond looking for an outlet but unable to find one. It seeks to destroy individualism. It is the worst crime to be perpetrated against humanity.

"Just because you can't see me or don't believe in me does not mean I don't exist. Just that you don't believe." In order to establish unity in the system, we must establish order. In this new age, we must join together in unity to forge a common bond of unity. We cannot allow the system or socialism to take over the church any more than it has. The very survival of this move of God on our country in revival depends on all of us working in unity. It is the time to act at forging unity. It is a shame that I see Christians now more worried about the end than the beginning. I see them acting as if I am not there. Talking it but not walking it, talking in my name, walking not in love, more worried about judging than loving. Miscasting people for who they are not and not for whom they are in order to gain from misrepresenting anything possible.

You have judged my apostles and prophets as if I did not know what I was doing. I don't want clones. I need individuals with heart and drive to finish the tasks given. I need people who have a dream that I, the Lord Yahovah, gave them to fulfill my way, not their own way that came from their own misguided heart. You must work with what you have been given by Yahovah or all you will have are old dreams with no substance. you must trust in the vision given to you by Yahovah and bring it to fulfillment.

Faith is not faith-based; it's faith or no faith at all. I walk by faith, not by sight. The Adonia commands with all your heart, all your might, and all your soul. I walk by the spirit and in the spirit. This is how you hear the voice of the great I Am. Yahshua is the sword of the spirit, which is the living word of the Torah. The word was revealed as the living Torah. I must be able to read and write the word to know the word. I know how to know and understand Yahovah, by reading and writing the word, which renews my mind daily. If I know the word, I can say the word Yahshua, the living son of Yahovah. To know the word, I must speak the word. To speak the word, I must walk the word. To walk the word, I must live the word. To live the word, I must die to self and deny all false religions and prophets.

I the great I Am has never sent a man that was illiterate of the word to anyone. All things must conform to the word of Yahovah and are subject to it. Yah had left a testament in rock of the living word of the Christ to disprove all religious false doctrines, such as the world is flat, the world is ten thousand years old, the sun revolves around the earth, etc.

I, Yahovah, will not live in any box that man has set up for me. I can do things any way I want. I am lord over you. I have set up laws in nature, just as I have for humans, that nature must obey and humans must obey or suffer the consequences. I will not disrespect the immutable laws that I have set up for all things to abide by, and they are contrary to all religious laws with no vision set up to control the public. I am not just a prophet. I am the living word, and anyone who has said this of me is the worst kind of false prophet, and you have followed a false religion that has no substance in me. The Living word Yahshua. It smells like rotten vinegar. Good wine put in the wrong vessel. It is the wrong wineskin. I, Yahovah, am the only true Yah, and my son is the living word made flesh, Yahshua, The living Christ. There are no substitutes for me. I have given you the choice to live or die without me.

JWG 2/1/11

THE EARTH WILL TRANSFORM INTO THE IMAGE OF THE CHRIST YAHSHUA

The earth will conform and transform to the image of the risen Christ Yashua. The earth is predestined to conform to the image of Yahovah's son, the living word, and not religion or false religious practices or false religious prophecy.

The earth is transforming before your very eyes and was set in transformation by Yahshua when he was slain for our sins. The earth is in the final transformation period of this time period. The earth is now in the birth pains of conforming its image and transforming into the image of the Christ it will become. It was formed by the Christ and must conform to the Christ's image. The earth and all of creation are resisting and struggling against the transformation period that will come to pass, and nothing will be able to stop it. Yah's new kingdom will come upon humanity, and nothing will or can stop it. Mankind is fighting it. The natural world is fighting it. The spirit world is fighting it. The angelic realm is fighting it.

All things will come into compliance and have been set in motion by Yahshua when he rose from the dead. The future is now becoming the present and then the past more rapidly than it ever has before. At this time in man's existence, the present and the future are colliding together at a rapid pace and are coming to a head. The law and the spirit fight against each other always. The bad foundations are being torn down and replaced with blessed foundations. You can't return to the law and walk by the spirit.

WAKE UP CALL

We also have the children of doom and gloom, those who wish they could return unto the earth and go green, but the only way you can truly do this is dead in the grave. I need new stewards of the new earth, stewards that will treat the earth as if it were alive and reborn and transformed. When I come, the first will become the last, heads will roll down my steps, and all the captives of this age will be set free. Heads will roll because when I come, heaven is coming with me and hell will follow my orders alone.

I have given you all a new wineskin to put the new wine in. Do not try to use the old wineskin. It will never work. It was flawed till I sent my son, Yahshua. The old wineskin will surely burst and only produce rotten vinegar every time you try to use it. New wine must be put in a new wineskin. This is why I have put you all in a newborn skin.

Repent and return to Yahovah.

JWG 4//7/11

THE SWORD OF YAHVAH
תֶּה סוּרִדּ פּ יְהֹשָׁה

Oh, chief general of the armies of the mighty Yahvah, look at how great the armies are that are arrayed against you. They are as far as the eye can see. They are vast and far too many for you to defeat. What will you do, sir, to defeat this great horde of evil arrayed in the valley of death below you? Oh, my great captains, hear my words. I do not need to look at any of their lost warriors or fallen heroes, for they are all dead in my eyes and by my hands! I will wipe the enemies of Yahovah off the face of the earth forever, and they will cease to exist forever. They will be lost in this valley of mine and cut off from receiving any help, and there will be no way of redemption for them.

The greater their numbers, the more will be given to the glory of Yahvah. Fear not the number or size of the host arrayed against you. Yahvah walks with you. The victory has been put in our hands by Yahvah. I promise they will all wish they had never come to this valley, and they will all not even have the time to repent of the deceitfulness and wickedness against Yahvah and his true prophets. Once they were good, but now they are all as good as dead in my mind, for now they will be dead forever.

Yahovah and his armies of angels and holy warriors are on our side, and through him we will do great signs and wonders as never seen before. Yah will not see us put to shame before our enemies any longer. So we will know the number that was once arrayed against us by the count of all their slain heroes and misguided warriors, fallen by our sides by our swords. We will make ready for battle and take no prisoners. "Oh, sword of Gideon, how keen and just of edge you are. How bright and just a blade you are and have always been. Yah sent you by his angels to me, his chief general on earth, and now I will lead legions of angels in his name that I see only with eyes of faith.

I thank you for all the lands and countries that I have and will conquer with this your sword, and it is an honor to have been deemed worthy to carry it in your holy name, Yahvah, and when I, James, have fulfilled my destiny and finished the work Yahovah has sent me to do, I will be able to stand guiltless and with pride in the halls of my forefathers at all the council fires, in the halls of all the princes, knights, warriors, and rangers of the most high Yah, for he has prepared a place for us, all the good, the bad, and the ugly. For some it will be a paradise; for others they will cease to exist forever, and their lying voices will never be heard again.

JHWG 11/7/11

ISIAH 58
HOW TO HONOR YEHOVAH IN TRUE WORSHIP

Shout out loud, don't hold back. Proclaim loudly like a trumpet. Tell my people what they have done against their Elohim; they still come looking for me to learn my ways. They act just like people that do what is right, that obey the commands of their Elohim. They ask to be judged fairly. They want Yahshua to stay near them. They say, "To honor Yehovah, we held special days and months when we gave up eating, but Yehovah didn't see or hear us. We humbled ourselves to honor Yahvah, but Yehovah didn't see or notice."

But this is what the Lord Yahvahshua says: "You do what pleases yourselves on these special days, and you are unfair to your workers. On these special days or months when you do not eat, you argue and fight and hit each other with your fists. You cannot continue to do things now as you have been doing them and believe that your prayers are heard in heaven. These are not the kind of special observances I want. This is not the way I want people to be sorry for their past sins. I don't want people to bow their heads like a plant and wear sackcloth and lie in ashes to mock some sort of sadness for past sin. This is what you do on your special days when you do not eat, but why do you think it is what the Lord Yehovah wants or needs?

"I will tell you what kind of special day I want: free the people that have been put in prisons unfairly and undo their chains. Free those to whom you have been unfair, and stop their hard labor. Share your food with the hungry, and bring poor homeless people into your home and churches. When you find someone in need of clothes, get them some, and stop refusing to help your relatives. Then your light will shine like the dawn, and your wounds will quickly heal.

"Your Lord Yahvahshua will walk before you, and the glory of the Lord Yehovah will protect you from behind. Then you will call out, and I, Yehovah, will protect and answer you. You will call out, and Yehovah will say, 'Hear I am.' If you will stop making trouble for others, if you stop using cruel words and pointing your finger at others, if you feed those that are hungry and take care of those who are troubled, then your light will shine on the darkness, and you will be bright like sunshine at noon.

"The Lord Yehovah will always lead you, Yehovah will satisfy your needs in dry lands and give strength to your bones. You will be like a garden that has much water, like a spring that never runs dry. You will rebuild what was in ruins. You will rebuild their foundations. You will be known for repairing the broken places and for rebuilding the land. You must obey the law of the Lord Yehovah and not do whatever pleases you on those holy days. You should call the Sabbath a holy, joyful day and honor it as the Lord Yehovah's holy day, the Sabbath. You should honor it by doing whatever you please or saying whatever you please on that day, then you will find joy in the Lord Yehovah, and I will carry you to high places above the earth. I will let you eat of crops you did not sow in the lands that your ancestors had." The Lord Yahvahshua has proclaimed these things.

PS

Hunger causes a broken spirit. If I, Yahovah, broke you once, I don't want to break you again and again. I want to dwell within you, so you must renew your mind and body daily with the Holy Spirit. This is the true worship and repentance. This is my only proclaimed fast and is the contrast between right and wrong worship. I want to renew your soul, spirit, and mind daily through a worshipful diet that renews the whole body in a spiritual way, not according to the added laws of men. You can be at the right place with the wrong frame of mind and continue making trips around the mountain. There is a big difference between walking the right path and knowing how to walk the path the right way. You can only walk this path with Yahshua and him alone and no other.

JWG 11/5/11

You are sworn to the spirit of all things.
Your heart knows only valor.
Your heart knows and follows only virtue.
Your always defend the helpless.
You might upholds the weak.
Your words are spoken in truth.
Your wrath will undo all the schemes of the wicked.
Remember your sixth sense.
Remember your discipline.
Remember your teaching.
Remember, you must control the eye of your mind.
Remember, you must utilize all your senses to overcome all things.
You will sense the blow before it falls; the bells chime before the bell is struck.

    You have withstood the thunder of the past and the fire of the present. Now you will leave with the wind of the future, and you will let the eye of your mind guide your steps in whatever may come upon your path.

12/10/11 JWG

THE NEW KNIGHT OF THE REALM

ט תֹה ר-לם
תֹה נוּ -ג כננהת

New knights I have chosen will arise
A knight is sworn to valor
His heart knows only virtue
His blade defends the helpless
His might upholds the weak
His words speak only truth
His wrath undoes the wicked
His shadow makes fear flee
His helmet is covered in mercy
His bow never misses its mark
His shield blocks all bows
His lance is like lightning
His voice is like thunder
His mouth doesn't sip the cup of vanity
His senses are one with soul and spirit
His eyes see all coming danger
His lips will always taste victory
His feet will carry all the hopeless
His glory he gives to the Lord Yahvah.

JWG 12/7/11

DECLARE

I saw Satan fall like lightning from heaven. I saw Satan fall. I saw Satan lose all. I saw all his works come falling down.
I saw all his angels fall by my sword.
I saw all his works come falling down.
I saw Satan come falling down like a rock with the rock of heaven.
I saw all his works come falling down.
I saw all his religious demons, warlocks, witches, groves, and all witchcraft, too, all came falling down. All came falling down in the name of Yahshua.
I saw it all. You are now paralyzed with all your works.
I saw it all. We have the victory and have won the war before it was started. I saw it all happen.
I saw Beelzebub fall like lightning from heaven.
I saw Babylon fall.
I saw all his demons fall.
I saw all the devil's guard fall by my sword from heaven.
We declare your time is over.
We declare your time is now over, and you are now chained is Sheol, with no escape. I saw you fall in my web, and you are now paralyzed, sorry.
I saw it all.
I saw Satan fall like lightning from heaven.
I saw Yahshua would arise.
I saw Yah arise.
I saw Yahvah arise.
I saw Yahovah arise.
Halleluyahvahshua.
I saw it all happen before my own eyes. I saw it all. I saw it all.
I saw it all with cloven tongues of fire. I saw you give it all up.
I declare it.

WAKE UP CALL

I saw him give it all up.
I saw Satan die, forever, and give it all up.
I saw it all happen, halleluyah.

12/15/11 JWG

PROPHESY

I hear the voice of one crying in the desert, "Prophesy, prophesy, prophesy, prepare ye, roar like a lion, for the Lion of Judah comes. Roar in tongues of cloven fire."
We prophesy, prepare yourself.
We prophesy, prepare yourself for the way of the Lord Yahvah.
We prophesy, prepare yourself for the way of the Lord.
We prophesy to this city, to this nation. Give it up now, devil.
Give it all up, give it all up, and all that you have stolen and then some.
The wealth must all be given up to us now. We prophesy to the north, to the south, to the east, to the west. Give it up, give it up, give it up, give it up, give it up. We crossed the river; now we take it all back.
We prophesy.
We take back the land.
We take back the souls.
We have overcome by the body and blood of the Lion of Judah and by the words of our testimonies.
We prophesy an open heaven.
We prophesy an open heaven.
We prophesy an open heaven.
We prophesy to the north, to the south, to the east, to the west.
We prophesy an open heaven.
We prophesy, roar it loudly like a trumpet.
Give it up, devil.
Give it up devil.
Give it up devil.
We prophesy, let your glory come.
Let your glory come.
We prophesy an open heaven.
We prophesy an open heaven.
We prophesy an open heaven.

WAKE UP CALL

Let your glory come.
Let your rain come.
Let your wealth come.
Let the miracles come.
Let the healing come.
We prophesy an open heaven.
We prophesy an open heaven.
We prophesy an open heaven.
Halleluyah, halleluyah.
Halleluyahvahshua.
We love you, Lord Yahvah.
We love you, Lord.
We love you, Lord.
We thank you, Lord, for an open heaven.
We thank you for an open heaven.
We thank you for an open heaven.
We prophesy,
Halleluyahvahshua, he will reign and rule in this nation and city forever.

JWG 12/12/11

WHO IS THAT GUY!

Who is that guy? Who is that masked man? A judge? A prophet? He is a true disciple of the living Christ and follows no false doctrines. A real apostle, and he was handpicked by Yahvah and has all the power promised to come to us from heaven to bring it to the earth.

They are apostles of the royal family of the mighty Yahvah. They wear crowns like wings and have swords that are on fire and pierce the darkness before them.

We don't like the way he looks through us! Put him to sleep!

He sees all things, and he sees when he sleeps, then he translates and does far greater things!

They disappear before our eyes when we try to follow.

Who does he think he is, speaking to me like that? I arrived with so many titles. I want to keep this pretty little Antichrist religious spirit inside me. How dare he cast it out of me so that I cannot operate in the name of the Antichrist any longer! He doesn't look the way I want him to look! We need to change him to look and lie like us!

He will receive no bribes, for he runs the bank and government, that all must do according to what they say. There is no head over them, but the Lord Yahvah himself.

We'll just put a blanket on him or he'll see everything that we've been doing all along to keep the war going on.

Been doing? Following the antichrist? Uh! Oh! He sees through all our blankets and then burns them.

What do we do now, oh great religious spirit that we love to worship! Who does he think he is coming to our club like that? We have strong brainwashed men to throw him out of our club, uh, church!

WAKE UP CALL

Uh! Oh! We can't touch him, lest we become sick with the virus from Yahvah and become saved! We'll just put him in the freezer so we can turn the boat in the opposite direction. How dare he stop us from capturing and burying all the survivors we gathered.

The freezer - he has melted!

We'll just put a blanket on him.

The blanket burned when we tried to throw it on him!

How dare he come to our club and stop us from putting gold sparkles in the air ducts and saying it was gold! We have a show to put on for our club, oh, place of phony worship.

What do we do to stop it, now! Ridicule him!

It doesn't work. He bends our pointed finger back at us. Then he picks the crap back up and slings one thousand times more on us.

Blackmail him!

It didn't work. Our tongues began to wither in our mouths, and now he has more on us than we have on him more crap piles on us daily because of our mischief, and he is laid blameless always.

We'll just make up bad names for him!

But now all the children run to him and say he came to save the day. Now we must bow down and worship him.

He will not allow it and says that you may only worship Yahvah, and him alone do you worship with no graven idols.

How do we get rid of him, for he has stopped us from robbing the poor and needy with fraud?

Send him on a mission.

It doesn't work on him. He's from God, the great and mighty Yahvah. He founded a newborn nation and a new monetary system based on cash, not ran by a bunch of governments of fraud.

Well it's easy, now call him a fraud snake oil salesman. That always works.

All of his cures and medicines work every time forever, and they only need to come to him once to be healed! He heals many every day forever out in the desert as was foretold.

We'll just say that, now, he speaks with lies and to the dead.

But he always tells the truth, and the truth will set us free of the religious spirit that has bound us, and everything happened as he said, and the very dead rose before us in golden armor to protect him.

We'll just act as if you can't see him and like he isn't there.

It didn't work. More and more and more come to him every day!

An army has now appeared out of nowhere, ten times as big as ours with all the armor of Yahvah on them on chariots driven by cherubim. He even has another witness with him that can do everything he can with an army just as big as his now is, and I hear there are six more with the same size armies or greater growing daily!

We'll just say he hears voices of spirits and is crazy.

But he only hears the real voice of Yahvah, which has not spoken for two thousand years, and makes us all run in fear and horror of eternal death when he speaks. Everything we say he can hear, so we cannot speak, lest he hear us. There is nothing we can do now but repent daily or die.

Nothing can stop it now. The new kingdom has already begun and is transforming before your eyes. A big crack has formed in our graven idol we worship daily. Our fake gods are also cracking and falling down. We can't hold them up anymore. There is nothing we can do now; he's unstoppable.

Well, he can't hold court in a time of war. Just keep the war going on and on and on.

The war is over. We have lost badly, even our lives forever. Our whole army has been surrounded, slaughtered, and captured. We must submit and repent to the newborn king and his emissaries or we will burn with our works.

We must now submit all the spoils to him now, that he might have mercy before judgment, and the time for him to start the process to judge and bring the court to order, in fact, is now at hand.

Uh-oh, he has sounded the anvil. Oh! No!

In his preliminary speech, he said he would abolish the rigged court of frauds and liars, he will judge the dead last because they repented first of all guilt.

Since it is all written in the Lion's book of Life in heaven, all altered evidences will be impermissible. He will need evidence from both parties to accuse. No false accusations allowed. In fact, they will get you put in his jail for a long, long time with no key and only one way in and no way out, for lying in his court, the court of no liars.

When Eliyah comes to your church, will you become fearful of him and why he came because he will not look the way you wanted him to look or were told he would look?

He will look like I, Yahvah, want him to look, a trillion dollars, and run the first international bank of Yahvah.

He will establish a new kingdom.

He is enough, is always enough, will always be enough, and will always look like me, because he is that guy.

JWG 11/22/11

My past is over!
My present has been secured by the living Christ Yahshua!
My future is set on the rock of my salvation!
My circumstances now have been overcome by Yahvah!

I AM A LIVING TREE

I am a living tree that has been planted on the bank firmly, by the rivers of living rainbow waters.

I was planted by Yahshua, and he supplies me.

Through Yahvah, the eternal river flows through the living rainbow of life.

The living rainbow flows through the eternal living waters of life, and all things that are alive flow through and into these rivers of eternal life-giving waters.

The cosmic rainbow of all life flows through all created things and is connected to these rivers of life that flow freely throughout the living earth.

They cannot be disrupted by the greed of men or his mischief.

They are all set in motion by Yahvah and are unstoppable.

The eternal wave flows in and out through these living waters of eternal life, perpetually, in the right season of time.

The flowers of the bows of my living trees bring forth good fruit with good seed every season.

They are pollinated by his bees, the living word of Yah.

The honey from these bows is the restored word of Yahvah.

I have no need to want or fear.

His rivers of eternal living waters will sustain me in the midst of all my needs and make me flourish and thrive.

His body and blood flow through the eternal living waters and have made me not guilty in the name of Yahshua the Christ.

His body and blood flow through my roots and make me whole.

My roots flow deeply into these living waters and produce new good fruit daily with good seeds.

These living waters of life flow into my veins and sustain me eternally.

The waters are disease-free, pure, and holy, and they sustain me daily.

I came from his seeds that he raised.

He planted me firmly on solid fertilized soil. Now my fruits fall into the river of life, from my bows, and flow onto good fertile soil on the banks of his holy river of life.

New saplings come from my holy seeds, and they will produce fruit in their own seasons.

I am now a great tree with living roots growing and flowing on the banks of the living rainbow river of life, the only eternal living waters.

I am now one of the rainbow river's living orchards.

Now my limbs and leaves shade the river to keep it temperate and pest-free.

The power of the living rainbow river now flows from my hands and body.

This flow will cause total incorruptible healing of your body and mind.

I am not a graft onto an old perishing root system.

I came from good seeds produced by Yahvah.

My roots are from good stock, and they are connected to this never-ending river of life.

I am an individual tree among many he planted firmly on the banks of the eternal living river of life.

I am an independent living tree, but I work in unity with all living things.

I wear a crown that he has given me freely, but I have laid it at his feet, for he sustains me, not the crown.

So I am subject to him for redeeming me of all my sins, because only he endured the unendurable for me, and I can't outlove him.

And so, then I am subject to my inner guide, the Holy Spirit of Yahvah.

And so, then ultimately and intimately, I am subject to Yahvah, Lord of all, forever for everything.

So now living tress that always produce good fruit in the right season are now surrounding me always.

JWG 5/16/12

TWENTY-FOUR OXEN ALL TOGETHER YOKED
בְּד צֶנֵ ־לִתגִתַתהֵר יִכָד

(1 Kings 19:19-21)

Elisha was plowing the fields with twelve yoked oxen, and he himself was behind the twelfth ox. This means there were twenty-four oxen all together yoked. A yoke takes two: it won't work any other way. Twelve came first, all equally yoked, then came Elisha then came twelve more equally yoked oxen- twenty-four burden bearers.

Elijah was Elisha's guide, a double portion, so when the prophet comes to you and places his mantle on you, you cannot walk away from it. He is your new guide, and if you do not follow his way, the way of Yahvah, you will surely die spiritually, forever.

You can only kiss your father and mother good-bye! Then you must kill what you used to use to supply all your needs. You alone must do it utterly and completely. You must prepare it, cook it, feed it, and then burn it all up as a sacrifice to Yahvah. This must be done spiritually, not physically. The prophet cannot do it for you. He can only help you in the process.

You can't go back to anything now. Yahvah will send you back in his strength, alone. You must go forward, never retreat! You must jog! You must tital! You must keep moving forward, taking ground in every move you make. In so doing, you are putting everything into the hands of Yahvah and his prophet.

So Yahvah alone starts supplying all your needs! Supernaturally! In so doing, gullibility is thrown in the gutter. Then you will discern and learn in the proper manner the ways of discernment.

You must do it when the prophet comes to you or you will miss out on your double blessing. You will always be trying to catch up to something that will just be out of reach until you walk with the prophet for a while.

You will not receive the mantle you strove for, because you didn't like the way it looked or your mom or dad or brother or wife talked you out of it because you have more important things to do, like sitting in the same closet doing the same thing again. Nothing again, but starving in a casket, wondering why you're still in the same place! Here I am, riding the same boat sinking in the sand. Here I am again, saying someone prophesied this and that!

What is defined as insanity, doing the same thing again and again, obtaining the same result? By one mingled word, I changed the true meaning of the phrase and quandary.

You must take time to walk with my prophet in my mountains, my wilderness, my valleys, my oceans; this is what I am, and where I am. I don't live in a box man has made for me to live in, and I never will again. I made all things, and this is where all my help comes from, the maker of all things, not religion. Man makes these things up!

You must become my disciple to do this thing. I sent them out two by two. Why do you think you can do it some other way than my way? This is like chasing after other gods!

You cannot mingle my words I give to you with other words that I did not give. They do not come from me, but they come from the belly of Sheol, the spirit of religion. I have always sent a gatherer first to restore hope. I have already sent twelve deliverers, twelve heroes, twelve prophets, and twelve apostles to you. But you all treated them with no respect and as you pleased because you don't agree with what Yahvah said through them or the words aren't right according to you. You have been put to sleep and cannot even see what Yahshua did or the way he did it.

You have rejected everyone I sent to you to awaken you, even my son. You won't even use his real name and wait needlessly for some other. So now you sit in a closet, denying the deliverer he has sent because he doesn't look like you wanted him to look or have the words and names being mingled to suit one king or another.

I have seen them all gathering. There are quite a few that are waiting to be judged, and some have been waiting a long, long time. There are many ways to deny the Christ and enter into judgment. The courtrooms are now full. All the halls grow to overflow as well, and the line to be judged goes out the door into the streets. All are waiting! Sorry! No seatbelt!

You're a very, very bad person. I need to take your car. You don't look insurable, so we will make it so you can't get it!

Job? What would a person want a job for or to work for? Pay? We'll only take half of what you make, and don't forget to tithe another 10 percent to your church clubhouse?

House? You don't need a house; it's the end. We'll just give it all away to an illegal, corrupt creditor who has no real, just, or valid claim on it. Ohh! Well, ah! Just go live in a cave or teepee.

Woe to you foolish ones! Awaken, all those that have fallen asleep.

Let me now check your farts and all your private parts too! It's okay! I'm just checking you out, not feeling you out. You could be normal, but for some reason, there's stuff in your pockets or belt or shoe or bra or panties or salsa or whatever I can think of next.

Unfortunately, there are still very few to none who seem to be finding the crooked, narrow pathway out of destruction. They must want to keep following lies because the truth hurts too much.

I don't want to feel any pain at all. It's way too hard to do it his way. I want to do it halfway. They do not even see it because it is right in their face all the time. They are all spiritually color-blind! It's the first sentence of the first verse of the first chapter.

He's not doing it the way we planned it to be. He's busting all our theories! He's overturned the tables and houses of all the money handlers! He made it so we don't have a job cleaning pee and crap off the streets anymore! He keeps tearing down our special little pretty idols we made for ourselves to worship instead of the Lord of all things, Yahvah.

We wouldn't want you to use any real names something might happen. You know who knows what could happen. The last will be first, and the first will be last. The last are first, and the first are last. In your mind, the last person you saw is the first person on your mind. So if the last person you saw at night was Yahshua, then the first person you will see in the morning is Yahshua. But that is only if your eyes are fixed on Yahshua and on the way Yahshua did it!

An apostle, one who has forsaken his old religious fake party doctrine to start a new nonreligious party doctrine with the risen Messiah. "Before my kingdom comes, I will restore my judges as at first and your counselors as in the beginning of Zion."

Now, son, you're supposed to have fun at a party, and it's always neutral ground supernaturally. No weapons allowed. You must check 'em at the door! Suits and dresses are required. Sorry! No exceptions! We'll even put one on you or take them off you.

JWG 1/24/12

IT IS HEREBY PROCLAIMED!

Only by the body and blood and through the body and blood of Yahshua, am I redeemed from the hands of the enemy!

Through the body and the blood of Yahshua, I am forgiven of all my sins, past and present!

Through the body and the blood of Yahshua, I am continually cleansed from all my sins!

Through the body and the blood of Yahshua, I am justified through Christ and made righteous as if I had never sinned!

Through the body and the blood of Yahshua, I am sanctified, made holy, and set apart in Yah!

Through the body and the blood of Yahshua, I am bold and can enter into the presence Yahvahshua!

Through the body and the blood of Yahshua, I am covered by the blood of Yahshua, and it cries out continually to Yah on my behalf!

Through the body and the blood of Yahshua, I am more than a conqueror. I am an overcomer!

Through the body and the blood of Yahshua, I am a warrior for the Christ!

Through the body and the blood of Yahshua, I am a disciple of the living Christ, and he is my friend.

Through the body and the blood of Yahshua, I have dominion over all things!

Through the body and the blood of Yahshua, I have been granted eternal life!

Through the body and the blood of Yahshua, my strength is continually renewed. I will dance and not grow weary, forever.

It takes the body and the blood to be made sinless—the body and blood of one son made into man by the one and only Yah.

I have been redeemed only by the body and blood of Yahshua. Otherwise you are receiving half instead of the whole thing, and maybe that's why it's only halfway working for you.

Yahshua didn't come to give you half. He came to give you the whole kingdom, not halfway. He went all the way for you on the cross.

So then, he already died on a cross—for you so you don't have to and are not required to.

You are required to do greater works than Yahshua did to help establish the new kingdom of Yahovah, greater works that no one has written about yet.

They choose to write doom and gloom and think they are going to float away instead of being gathered to the garner of Yahovah.

Yahovah needs living people to procreate the new kingdom of Yahovah.

The rapture is the biggest farce ever perpetrated on the public, besides Islamic Baalism.

It's simple. Spirits need a body to live in or they are just a spirit.

Yahovah is the father of all spirit, so then only Yahovah is something more than a spirit. He is the father of all life.

Amen. Selah.

JWG 11/29/10

WAKE UP CALL

Your ministry has been numbered and weighed upon scales and found to be deficient of love. Your ministry will be divided and given over to those whom you have thrown away.

mene', mene',
>*tekel,*

>>*upharsin*

    Your ministry has been numbered and been weighed upon the scales!
    It has been found to be deficient of love!
    Your ministry will be divided and given over to those whom you have thrown away!

>>>Yahshua

HIS PRELIMINARY SPEECH
הִס פֶּרְלִמְנְ־רִי ספפשה

The chief judge of all the judges has stated this for his first preliminary speech to all the nations of his world.

Beware, lawyers, for lying. You will receive disbarment and life in my jail forever immediately and without any recourse. All false charges will be dealt with in the same manner.

A false witness is an abomination to Yahvah. Marriage is holy and for life. If you marry to steal, you will receive the same reward as a thief receives.

I, Yahvah, allowed men to have more than one wife because there was a need for man to have more help to build an everlasting family. Children are a sign of wealth. This is why I gave women to men. Men and women have abused this privilege.

It is an honor for a woman to bring new life into the world, and they will not dishonor that honor I, Yahvah, gave them to perform.

No one will not say I, Yahovah Adonia, made a mistake; I make no mistakes with any life or anything. I am the only spirit that is perfect in every way. Marriage is between a man and a woman, and no other. There is nothing to discuss. When marriages and partnerships come to a separation and things must come to a division, all things will be divided equally and fairly between both parties.

The misuse of governmental powers for their own private gains will not be tolerated any longer.

You work for me and the people. This is your legacy; this is your only agenda.

You will no longer come in with your own dumbass religious political agendas that are destroying my nation that stands for me, the Christ Yahshua.

You will not socialize my nation.

You are not to be the monkey on the people's backs any longer.

This includes all police departments; all fire departments; all judicial courts of all cities; counties, states, countries; all three governmental forms of the US government, the judicial branch, the executive branch, and the legislative branch; and the pentagon.

You work for the people, not your watch commanders.

You are not here to regulate the public out of existence with fraudulent taxation and continual overregulation of the public and no regulation of those that are in this country fraudulently or the fraudulent leadership that wishes to harm this nation under Yahvah.

You, all of you in leadership, have been stealing from the public with the worst phony scam ever thought up, and like a dumbass, you follow along like a bunch of lemmings and continue to rape and steal from the public till there is nothing left for you to steal but a ghost town. You don't go along with the crap in the pigpen; you wash it all out.

It's time to clean out all the whitewashed walls and rooms of my house under Yahvah.

I will wash my house clean. Whitewash is used to cover up the fact that you have done nothing to help the public or to fix a thing.

You do not know what the meaning of public servant is.

You have given them whitewash.

Lying is lying. Sorry! The time is coming when I will have no more mercy for you.

If you can't form a uniform code of justice for the people, then I will enforce Yahshua's uniform code of justice for all, not some.

If it is found that you have committed a grievous offense to the citizens by fraudulent actions, money laundering, misappropriation of funds, coercion, conflict of interest, etc., you will be tried and judged in the court of the most high Yahovah! You will be interned at the lake of fire to burn for eternity.

3/21/13 JWG, the Naked Prophet

LET US DO WHAT WE WERE BORN TO DO!

Let us understand the situation we are faced with! We are ordered into battle against a tough and determined enemy and army.

I can't promise to bring home all alive as we walk through the valley of the shadow of death. But I promise I will be the first on the mountain or valley battlefield floor and the last to step off the battlefield, and I will leave no one behind! Dead or alive, we will all come home together! I will leave no one behind that follows Yahshua into this battle!

You have become a soldier in the greatest armies ever formed in the universe—a soldier in the armies of the living Christ Yahshua!

No one will be left behind! We will defeat this enemy, because we walk with Yahshua to bring in his new kingdom on earth!

To inspire your men, you have to be with them! I, Yahshua, walk with my apostles!

Halleluyahvahshua! Selah.

It is finished!

10/31/13

THE LORD YAHOVAH'S VENGEANCE WILL BE THEIR PAIN NOW!

I made you a son. You are who you are now, but that doesn't mean you have to do what they want you to do!

You are my servant now! You will follow me, and me alone will you follow!

The war between heaven and hell is finished. Yahshua finished it!

We now are in the process of removing all the rable from the pit for final removal, forever!

The lost seek to keep the war going on and on to try to stop judgment from falling on them, when it is over and finished!

This is my war, not yours!

You defy the beast of false religion!

You tear down all the walls of the beast in every arena!

I defy the image of the beast, and I raise up leaders that will defy the image of religiosity and the beast! You are here to fight the image of the beast in all the atmospheres!

I saw Hasatan die and fall from heaven! I saw Livyatan the beast die and get shattered in irreparable pieces! I saw all the demonic principalities fall from heaven into the pit prepared for them all to burn!

I command the earth to conform to the image of Yahshua, the only Christ Messiah! I take dominion over all things visible and invisible! I am dominion, and I rise up with Christ Yahshua and take dominion over all things! I have dominion over money! Money has no dominion over me! It doesn't take money; it takes eyes of great faith!

The war between good and evil depends on the choices we make, and those choices take personal sacrifices! Simply your undivided mind and heart!

WAKE UP CALL

You must believe without doubt! It doesn't matter what they think! It matters what you think! You must believe you have the strength and power of Yahovah! The zeal of Yahvah's house will consume all things that try to come against you!

You have been using your armor and gifting by reflex motion! You will gain spontaneous control to manifest the new kingdom on earth! You must learn to manifest and control your God-given power at all times!

It is a living extension, through you, of the manifested power of Yahovah! Your own human instincts mixed with the Holy Spirit translating your thoughts and power into living reality!

The power of a son of Yahovah! You must visualize the objective given clearly to manifest it into living physical reality!

Anger is your downfall! Do it with unquenchable love! Apostle of Yahovah, concentrate on the tasks at hand, not the spells they try to cast upon or against you! Their spells will become void and will be multiplied back upon them that try to come against you!

All my heroes are dead and gone to heaven, but inside of me, the power of Yahshua lives on and on. It's a long, hard road coming back from the closed gates of hell, and Yahshua finished it when he killed and defeated Hasatan and Livyatan in hell and took the keys to Sheol and closed it all down, released the captives, and interned all who followed Hasatan and Livyatan into the pit to be consumed forever. To some, I am but a sweet dream; to others I am their ultimate nightmare!

I command the forces of the universe to work for me! I am not going to do the things I am expected to do anymore! I am going to do the unexpected! The Lord Yahovah's love and vengeance will be the pain of the lost now!

Change your attitude and latitude! My speaking of this word of Yahovah creates the wave across the wavelengths, dimensions, and atmospheres that will wash this earth clean! The wave that will part all seas and wash away all the sides of doubt! I, Yahshua, have given you a new wineskin to put the new wine in. Don't try to use the old one; it is no good anymore, fit only for the dung heap!

11/27/13

ON THAT DAY, A PLEASANT VINEYARD WILL ARISE SING ABOUT IT

וְלֵיל ־דְסַ ־דְסַ סַנּוּ ־בַּתָ ת
נ ת־הת ד־י ־ פל־ס־נת שְׁנִי־דִד

The way of the righteous is level; righteous one, you smooth the path of the righteous.

Following the ways of your judgments, we put our hope in you. The desire of all our souls is to remember you and your holy name, Yahovah. My soul desires you at night. My spirit in me seeks you at dawn, for when your judgments are here on earth, the people on earth learn what righteousness is. Even if pity is shown to the wicked, he still will not learn what righteousness is. In a land of uprightness, he will still act wrongly and fail to see the majesty of his father Yahovah.

Yahovah Adonia, you raised your hand, but they still did not see. Yet with shame, they will see your zeal for your people. Yes, fire will destroy your enemies.

Yahovah Adonia, you will grant us peace; because all we have done, you have done for us.

Yahovah Adonia, our only Yah, other lords besides you have ruled us, but only you do we invoke by your holy name every day.

The lost dead will not live again. The lost demonic ghosts will not rise again, for you punished and destroyed them once and for all. You have wiped out all memory of them and their seed forever.

WAKE UP CALL

You enlarged our nation, Father, Yahovah Adonia. Your glory and power enlarged the nation, and thus you have glorified yourself. You have extended all the frontiers of your nation.

Father, Yahovah Adonia, when leaders were troubled, they sought you. When you chastened them, they sought you. They poured out a silent prayer as a pregnant woman about to give birth cries out and writhes in her labor pains, so we have been at your presence, Yahovah Adonia, our father. We have been pregnant and been in pain. But we have given birth to wind and gas; we have not brought salvation to the land, and those inhabiting the world have not come to life.

Your dead will live. My corpse will rise again to my father, Yahovah Adonia. Awaken and sing, yes, those who dwell in the dust will awaken and sing, for the dew is like morning dew, and the earth will bring its ghosts to everlasting life.

Come, my people, enter your rooms. Shut your doors behind you. Hide yourselves for a little while until the wrath of Yahovah is past. For see, my father, Yahovah Adonia, emerges and arises from his place of peace to punish those leaders on earth for their sins against him and their citizens.

Then the earth will reveal all the bloodshed upon it and no longer conceal all its slain.

On that day, my father, Yahovah Adonia, with his great, strong, relentless sword, will punish Livyatan, the fleeing serpent beast, the twisting shape-changing serpent beast Livyatan. My father, Adonia, will slay that sea of beasts.

On that day, a pleasant vineyard will arise. Sing about it, son. I, Yahovah Adonia, your father, guard it. Moment by moment I water it so that no harm will come to it. I guard it night and day.

I have no anger in me. If it gives me briars and thorns, then as in war, I will trample it all down and burn it up all at once so that it does not take hold of my strength, in order to make peace with me, yes, to make peace with me, Yahovah, your father, when there will be no peace given to that beast.

The time is coming when Yahshua will take root and Israel's flower will bud, and the religious beast will cease to exist in Israel any longer.

1/20/14 Isaiah 27:1

PSALM 17
פּסּ-לם בז

I, Yahovah, have heard your righteous pleas and given ear to your cries, and I have listened to your prayers!

They did not rise from deceitful lips! Your vindication has come from me, your Father in heaven!

You have seen what is right!

My son, I, Yahovah, have probed your heart and examined you at night and have tested you and have found nothing against you! Because you have resolved that you would not sin against your only Yah with your mouth!

As for your deeds, you have kept yourself from the ways of the violent!

Your steps have held to my pathways, and I will not allow your feet to slip from them!

I, Yahovah, have answered you and given ear to your prayers and heard them!

I will show you the great wonders of my love, for I have saved all with my right hand and given you all refuge from all your foes!

I will keep you as the apple of my eyes, and I will hide you under the shadow of my great wings from all the wicked that assail you and all your mortal enemies that have tried to surround you!

They all have closed up their callous hearts, and their mouths always speak in arrogance.

They have tried to track me down; they try to surround me, with their eyes ready to throw me to the ground.

They are like hungry lions for prey, like a great lion crouching in cover. I will rise up, says Yahovah, confront them and bring them all down to the pit.

WAKE UP CALL

I will rescue you from the wicked with my sword!

I, Yahovah, with my hand, will save you from the wicked men of this world, whose reward was in this life. I will still the hunger of those you cherish, and your sons and daughters will have plenty and store up wealth for themselves and their children's children.

You have seen my face in righteousness, and I have seen yours. I have awakened you to be satisfied with seeing my likeness.

Each time I awaken you, you will see my face!

I, Yahovah, will call you my son!

11/14/13

THE TWELVE COMMANDMENTS

The A-L Commandments

And so Moshe came down from the mountain of Yahovah and said, "The great I Am has made these commands for all to observe in reverence of I Am."

א = Alef = A— I am Yahovah Adonia, your only Yah, who brought you out of slavery.

ב = Beth = B— you are to have no other false gods before me. You are not to make for yourselves a carved image or any kind of representation of anything in heaven above, on the earth beneath, or in the water below the shoreline. You are not to bow down to them or serve them, for I, Yahovah Adonia, your Yah, am a jealous Yah, punishing the children for the sins of the parents to the third and fourth generations of those who hate me and my son, but displaying grace to the thousandth generation of those who obey my living word.

ג = Gimel = G— you are not to use dishonorably the name of Yahovah Adonia, your Yah, because Yahovah Adonia will not leave unpunished someone who uses his name carelessly without honor or removes it from the word out of religiosity.

ד = Dalet = D—

ה = He = H—

ו = Vav = W—
ז = Zayin = Z—
ח = Het, Cheth = J, CH—
ט = Tet, Teth = F—

י = Yod = Y—

כ = Kaf = K —

ל = La'med = L—

work and remember the day I am rested and set it apart to Yahvah. Priests have six days to labor and do all your work, but one day is a Shabbat for Yahovah Adonia, your Yah. On it priests are to do little work. For in six days Yahvah made heaven and earth, and on the seventh day, Yahovah rested. This is why Yahvah blessed that day and separated it for himself only. Do what must be done, and take your rest in Yahovah and his son, Yahshua.

honor your father and your mother so that you my live long in the land that Yahovah Adonia has given you.

you do not murder.

you do not commit adultery.

you do not steal.

you do not give false evidence against your neighbor. A false witness is an abomination before Yahovah.

you do not covet your neighbor's house; do not covet your neighbor's wife, his male or female slave, his ox, his donkey, or anything that belongs to your neighbor.

abide in my love, and love your brother as yourself, and the second is like unto this one.

love one another as I have loved you.

SONS AND DAUGHTERS OF YAHVAH

To, my sons and daughters, sons and daughters of Yahvah, sons and daughters of zion and The New Kingdom of Yahovah, so now, this is what the great I am, is going to do in your life.

So now, I will start activating all your hidden gifts that you alone were born with. The gifts I gave you and only I can give you!

I will renew your strength and keep you in the palm of my hand.

You will always have the youthfulness of a youngster and your handsomeness or beauty will never fail you!

You are a chosen risen warrior of Yahovah! Your arrows will pierce the heart with my arrow threw it! your voice will have the power to pierce heart with the unquenchable love of Yahovah.

You have been given the whole tool box at your disposal to use and create miracles and manifest the power of Yahovah on earth as it is in heaven!

You will have my blessing, favor and grace upon you and know one can stop you or curse you in any way!

No form of demonic witchcraft will be able to attach itself to you!

All their voodoo will come back on them force multiplied. No thing and no one can hurt you or harm you, nothing, for you have ten of my finest imperial guard arch angles at your side, to light, to guard, to rule, to watch over your house and to guide you!

The fear of Yahvah will come on anyone or thing that tries to hinder you or harm you in any way.

I am that I am and I am teaching you to walk with me in my love outside the box of socialism, religion and religiosity!

WAKE UP CALL

I am, never formed a religion of men and socialism. they are not based on the love of one another as thy self, but in greed and slavery of the masses to corporatography.

You must love me more than the blessing!

My love is your greatest gift. From me Yahovah, Yahshua, and the Ruauch Ha Ka'deesh are my trinity of love, for you!

You will hear the sound of my voice clearly!

You will know the sound of my voice for it will sound just like yours, but with the answer to your question and solution to the problem at hand!

Because, now, sons and daughters 1 and you and you and I are now one!

I will walk with you if you will walk with me alone and not the demonic spirit of religion!

Together, we will walk threw the storms and I will supply all your needs, supernaturally.

Please don't worry about it and if you do the angels will say don't worry your in the palm of Yahovah's hand!

You will continue in youthfulness and childlikeness beyond 120 years, like Moshe or Sarah, because my handsome beauty favor and grace is upon you always and never shuts off!

What you have always dreamed and thought is true, because, I Yahovah gave you those thoughts and dreams and visions to complete, because I Yahshua saw you complete them all!

This day here by proclaimed by, James Garner, the real naked prophet JWG 12/21/12

PS. you are a star in Yahova's play!

THE COMPARISION OF HUMAN BEINGS AND OR PRIMATES

First of all, a real and true theory must be based on facts, not the altered falsification of facts to fit a thesis or supposed fake scenarios for notoriety, and it must be based on real information on the pre-history of the human species, not falsified specimens and documents.

The real facts that a human being must look at and state first as a basis or foundation to work upon are very few, altered and singularly unconvincing, and are useless as original data from which to draw any accurate conclusions because of these falsifications and misinterpretations, and the theory was proposed before DNA testing of these animals, chimpanzee's, apes, Neanderthals was available.

So then, this theory was formed with no genetic testing whatsoever having been performed and was only based on flattened falsified bone fragments from various animals, not humans.

All supposed prehuman skulls have been proven fakes. All humans have a unique brain structure and nervous system containing a soul that needs rest and a spirit from Yahovah that never sleeps, and that spirit is linked to Yahovah himself as a son or daughter of his universe. Your brain, thorax, and heart are uniquely interlocked, unlike an animal.

You have the choice to act like a human being or falsify yourself into an ape. You have adequate brain power to see the true light, and you were not given the brain of an animal to act like one. You were given the unique brain of a human being, that of a son of Yahovah himself, with all the subordinate power a son of the king has. The so-called Cro-Magnon man is the skeleton of a hardy human being that lived fully exposed to all the elements and is unchanged and identical to the human skeleton of today.

The false presumption of evolution is a mocking bogus counterfeit hypothesis and whose author, Charles Darwin, rebuked as an untenable theory. Archeologists trying to disprove creation developed evolution as a theory later on by using evolution to form a false narrative and to form false and misrepresented facts to fit a false hypothesis, and they falsified narrations and pictorial suggestions to lure the public into a false evolutionary belief system of scientific quackery, when all the facts that support that false theory have been proven to be faked and manipulated to suit their theory, which tries to disprove the fact that humans were created by the Holy Spirit from the earth, fire, air, and water of our planet and put here by Yahovah, the great spirit and are not some mutated accidental incident.

All planets in the universe evolve, but that does not mean life forms evolve outside of the basic parameters set up by Yahovah himself so that there would be no cross-contamination of the initial life forms created by Yahovah himself.

The false Darwinian presumption of evolution of the apes to a human being is that during the development of the human being, through various intermediate unrelated missing links that have never been found, a human could be traced back to those cell-like formations that are the original types of life known to us, which is a false presumption. And then at the same time, we are disposed to assert that some antediluvian jellyfish away back in the past ages developed a human brain, crawled out of the water, and somehow became the making of the first human being.

How big of a fairy tale can I make up to gain notoriety? All those presumptions with no facts to back anything up at all is as Darwin said—untenable.

Evolution is the creation of a falsified narrative to support a falsified, bogus, bigoted, racist theory. Yahovah is the creator of all things in this universe, and he himself invented science and mathematics and everything else there is that exists. Evolution is not a love, and you were created from love, not a mutated accident.

The evolution of primates is a counterfeit theory based on bogus, fake facts and the manipulation of bone fragments to present a fake hypothesis based on falsified information and falsified bone parts from other animals to support and make a supposed complete skeleton, but is a totally incomplete skeleton falsified to fit a falsified hypothesis.

A theory of falsified facts, when you can't find them, you make them up or find parts from some other sources or animals to fit your bogus theory of falsified facts to fit a supposed scientific agenda. It is a prime example of archeology gone awry to fake a falsely believed theory and agenda, even when the facts prove otherwise or are falsified to fit the hypothesis, in order to gain money and notoriety from deception.

So simply, evolutionary archeology scientists fill in the missing parts, or flattened part or parts of bone with what they want the specimen to look like, then discredit all scientists that don't follow along or agree with their bogus narrative and false theory of misrepresented facts. They are brainwashed by the hypnosis of the real facts that are in front of themselves. No complete skull or body has ever been found of these supposed hypothetical races of chimpanzee. When you assume, you make a monkey out of me and you and you and me.

It is racist to assume certain or any humans evolved from apes. Oh, and don't say you're black or white, but say you're the product of an ape and not a son of the one and only Yahovah. How satanic and bigoted can you make it?

Antichrist is Antichrist. No matter how many pretty bows and ribbons you put on the pig, it's still a pig.

The evolution of all creations is a bogus intangible theory, which tries to take Yahovah out of the picture but can't because the Holy Spirit created it all outside of what you call time and space, by the spirit, from another dimension of time and space, into the reality of what is today.

You are created sons and daughters of Yahovah himself, created to be a cut above an angel, not an ape. Creation is a tangible, sustainable fact, not an unsustainable theory of falsified facts.

So then, to say you have heritage with an ape brings in deception and dissension and tries to disclaim, derogate, demean, and dishonor Yahovah, Yahshua, his holy word, the Holy Spirit, and all his angels and risen warriors and breaks the third of the twelve commandments given by Yahovah and Yahshua.

You are not to use lightly the name and/or word of Yahovah Adonia, your Yah, nor remove his name from any scripture out of religiosity, because Yahovah Adonia will not leave unpunished someone who dishonors the name or word of Yahovah.

It has been proven by the DNA, genetically, that it is impossible for a human being to be related to an ape or any so-called prehuman, not even a Neanderthal. To get a perfect example of divine inheritance, you must look at human mitochondrial DNA and the genetic code. The main problem of evolution is that it is a proposed process that always runs into a genetic dead end and leaves gigantism and dwarfism unexplained or a disease. The real facts should be stated first as a real basis to work upon, but there are no facts. The ones I am presented are altered and singularly unconvincing and are useless as facts or original data from which to draw a proper conclusion or evolutionary thesis, because of all the altered specimens and falsified fake skulls and no DNA or genetic testing whatsoever.

From all human genes, the female genetics can be traced back fifteen thousand years. Despite thousands and thousands of years of human existence, there is very little variation among the six billion on earth living today. Humans are the most unusual species in this world, which Yahovah created, in that of our own distinct individual human genetic code composition compared with all the other created species of the earth.

So then, human beings have their own separate genetic code, as do all other life forms created by Yahovah, a separate code for each species.

When we look at the real unmanipulated facts, we find that humans from as far apart as the Eskimos in Alaska, Europeans, Asian, the Egyptians in Egypt, and the Aborigines in Australia are genetically more similar to each other than two chimpanzees from the same social group in the same jungle of West Africa and could never have crossed or procreated with any other primate or so-called prehuman chimpanzee. So then, only the facts about creation by an all-knowing great spirit that created all things and governs the whole universe should prevail. Only one true living yah would cause such limited genetic diversity and a code for each species.

Geneticists have reconstructed a population of about five thousand breeding females from the last great volcanic eruption about seventy thousand years ago before the flood ten thousand years ago, that all humans on earth that exist or existed are related to this one and only genetic bottleneck that makes them all sons of Yahovah, rooted with Adam and Eve.

Humans have always been omnivorous and do not and cannot eat the diet of an ape and stay physically healthy. Recently found human bones in North Africa from fifteen thousand years ago, before the Great Flood, showed signs of tooth decay from a sugary diet of oats and honey and meats. This suggests the facts that they grew and stored food and made beer and ate meat since all were plentiful then. They stored food year round and were in touch with the earth's cycles and calendar days, because they even stored nuts and honey.

All this contradicts bogusly held religious and evolutionary false beliefs and interpretations about all early humans, even Neanderthals that have already been proven to not be related in any way to a human and could never have in any way procreated with a human being. They are more likely what was called a troll. All early fossils supposed as prehuman, such as Piltdown and Java man, have all been proven to be fakes to fake a fake evolutionary process that does not exist. All supposed prehuman skulls have been proven as a hoax to further the false theory of evolution and are skulls from large chimpanzees, and no full skulls or bodies have ever been found of any prehuman. The theory is based on some flattened bone fragments that are not enough to complete a full skull or correct body structure and some other faked large chimpanzee's skull parts, which are skulls of primates and not human in any way, and some so-called missing link that has been proven bogus by genetics.

So then, we have a faked theory developed to prove evolution, but in the process, it disproves evolution. They have developed a whole species from one set of incomplete bone fragments that are not enough bone fragments to create a whole species from. One chimpanzee bone fragment is not enough evidence to create a whole race of prehumans.

By all the present facts, evolution is a bogus theory of a chimpanzee evolving from an amoeba then into a thinking rational life form. If chimpanzees were part of an evolutionary process, there would be no chimpanzees left on earth now, because they all would have evolved into a higher life form. This is the biggest scandal and fairy tale ever told to mankind and was proposed by a bigot that believed Africans were a race of subhuman. For some reason, human beings have been misled to believe this as fact, when all the facts lead to the contrary fact, that either we were put here by Yahovah or created here by Yahovah.

Get it clearer.

All things exist and work according to Yahovah's power, rule, and authority, not supposed theories. So then, what came first, the two chickens that made the fertilized egg, or two fertilized eggs appeared from nowhere and then procreated the whole earth? This is the problem with an untenable theory, which is unsustainable by any and all means and is based upon monetary gains and not the real facts at hand.

5/21/14

AT THE BEGINNING OF THE NEW AGE

AT THE BEGINNING OF THE NEW AGE OF AQUARIUS WAS A VERY DELICATE TIME.

The kingdom of yahovah began appearing on earth from another dimension of time and space, threw the frontiers of heaven.

It is a place that lies between the summit of men's dreams and knowledge and the pit that all humans fear to fall in, it is the dimension of dreams and imagination.

The courthouse was established first and called to order to clear the line in heaven.

Most were unaware of its arrival and more willing to follow false prophecies from false prophets that never accepted apostolic Order, even when a risen. emissary, nazarite, apostle, priest chosen from the order of melchizedek, came to announce the kings coming and arrival. He has commanded that every citizen of America will be given 170,000 as part of "the sower plan" stimulus package and then taxed 70,000 to pay Off the nation's debt in one year and stimulate the whole world's economy.

He established a new treasury and abolished derogatory departments of the government no longer needed.

KNOW NOW THEN IT IS THE YEAR 2014, THE EARTH IS BEING RULED BY COUNTRIES DISGUISED AS CORPORATIONS and CORPORATIONS DISGUISED AS COUNTRIES, BUT WITH BLIND ARMIES OF POLITICAL SLAVES, WHILE INSTALLING THE MACHINES AND leaving the public clueless and in slavery to the hypnotizing machines they have created to hypnotize the public into a state of walking sleep. While they glean information from the citizens to hypnotize them even further with whatever their desire it is to find. While trying to keep most citizens living from paycheck to paycheck or without a paycheck, the most precious substances have become fossil energy, green energy, a computer, a laptop, a phone or ipad, gold, water, drugs, alcohol, sex and whatever fad they can pull on the public without the government or corporations noticing the scam.

A COMMAND FROM YAHVAH IS NOT A SUGGESTION.
5/21/16

DIMENTIONAL TRAVELING

The first step is giving The Holy Trinity your whole undivided heart then Yahovah, Yahshua and the Ruauch Ha Kaddish, the holy trinity, will start expanding a humans consciousness to a higher level and dimension.

This means your whole and undivided heart.

The trinity extends life and is vital to portal dimensional travel and translation thru time and space and all navigation thru it.

Yahovah has given me the ability to fold time and space and 1 have gained the ability to travel and navigate threw it, from one point to another, while stationary, without moving, but dimensionally moving threw time and space.

It is the ability to translate and travel to any part of the universe and return safely without having to move or walk in real time.

Oh! yes!

So then we begin folding time from one interdimensional point, to another interdimensional point of time.

DON'T WORRY
BE HAPPY

Don't Worry! Everything is going to be ok!
    STOP!
    Done Worry! Be Happy!
    Everything's Goin'na Be Ok!
    STOP! Be Happy! Don't Worry!
    No Reason To Fear Anything At All Today!
    It's Goin'na Be A Good Day Today and Everyday!
    No Reason To Fear Anything!
    I AM, Is In Charge Of It All Today!
    So! Hey! Its Goin'na Be A Happy Day!
    Everything's Goin'ta Go His way! La! La! La! Da! Da! Da!

HOLY ANOINTING OIL

HOLY ANOINTING OIL FLOW OVER MY SOUL, BY YOUR BODY AND BLOOD YOU COVER ME, BY YOUR LOVE AND GRACE 1 AM FREE, BY YOUR LOVE YOU SHELTER ME AND COMFORT ME, HAVE THE HEALING POWER OF YOUR TEMPLES RIVERS FLOW OVER MY SOUL AND SPIRIT, REFRESH MY MIND AND BODY, WITH THE HEALING POWER OF YOUR LIVING WATERS, HAVE YOUR HEALING POWER FLOW OVER MY SPIRIT AND SOUL EMPOWER MY MIND AND BODY

RIGHT NOW, YAHSHUA YAMLEKH, LET THE RIVERS OF YAHOVAH ABDIEL ADONIA'S NEW KINGDOM FLOW OVER MY BODY AND SOUL AND BRING IN YOUR HEALING POWER AND LOVE OVER MY EARTH, RIGHT NOW, YAHSHUA HADADRIMMON, BURST THE POMEGRANATE, FULFILL YOUR PROPHECIES, DESTROY THE TWINS OF POVERTY AND GREED, WAS MADE FOR YOUR BATTLE. I, YAHOVAH, FULFILL YOUR PROPHECIES RIGHT NOW THREW ME YOUR VESSEL OF STRENGTH!

HAVE THE RIVERS OF YAHOVAH'S LOVE AND GRACE FLOW OVER YOUR EARTH!

OH EL-OHIM, LET YAHOVAH ABDIEL ADONIA, ARISE IN YOU!

ALL YOUR ENEMIES WILL SCATTER, AT THE SOUND OF YOUR REAL NAME.

YAHSHUA YAMLEKH, YOU WILL BE MADE TO REIGN ON EARTH AS IT IS IN HEAVEN AND YOUR KINGDOM NOW COMES AS YOU PROPHESIED ON EARTH.

JWG 4/23/14

I WILL CHANGE YOUR NAME TO SON OF THE LIVING YAHOVAH!

I HAVE CHANGED YOUR NAME. YOU WILL NO LONGER BE CALLED, WOUNDED, OUTAST, LONELY OR AFRAID, I HAVE CHANGED YOUR NAME, YOUR NEW NAME WILL BE, CONFIDENCE, JOYFULNESS, LOYALTY, THE LOYAL ONE WHO SEEKS MY FACE. 1 HAVE CHANGED YOUR NAME, YOUR NEW NAME WILL BE, FAITHFULNESS, RIGHTEOUSNESS, JUSTICE, LOYALTY, SON OF THE LIVING YAH.

I HAVE CHANGED YOUR NAME, GIVEN YOU A CROWN, AND CALLED YOU MY SON.

I HAVE CHANGED YOUR NAME, I WILL TAKE YOU BY THE HAND AND WALK WITH YOU INTO THE PROMISED LAND TO BUILD THE NEW KINGDOM OF YAH, ACCORDING TO YAHOVAH'S PLANS.

I WILL COME WITH FIRE IN MY EYES AND THE POINT OF GRACE IN MY HANDS.

I WILL COME AGAIN AND ESTABLISH MY APOSTOLIC KINGDOM ON EARTH AS IT IS IN HEAVEN.

I WILL ESTABLISH MY NEW KINGDOM KNIGHT HERO APOSTOLIC JUDGES AS AT THE BEGINNING.

I WILL JUDGE THE QUICKENED FROM THE DEAD AND THE DEAD IN CHRIST YAHSHUA WILL RISE INTO HIS ARMY OF RISEN WARRIORS, THAT WILL LIVE FOREVER WITH HIM. AMEN

I AM A LIVING TREE

I AM A LIVING TREE THAT HAS BEEN PLANTED ON THE BANK FIRMLY, BY THE RIVERS OF LIVING RAINBOW WATERS. I WAS PLANTED BY YAHSHUA AND HE SUPPLIES ME.

THROUGH YAHVAH, THE ETERNAL RIVER FLOWS THROUGH THE LIVING RAINBOW OF ALL LIFE.

THE LIVING RAINBOW FLOWS THREW THE ETERNAL LIVING WATERS OF LIFE AND ALL THINGS THAT ARE ALIVE FLOWTHREW AND INTO THESE RIVERS OF ETERNAL LIFE GIVING WATERS.

THE COSMIC RAINBOW OF ALL LIFE FLOWS THREW ALL CREATED THINGS AND IS CONNECTED TO THESE RIVERS OF LIFE THAT FLOW FREELY THROUGHOUT THE LIVING FARTH.

THEY CANNOT BE DISRUPTED BY THE GREED OF MEN OR HIS MISCHIEF. THEY ARE ALL SET IN MOTION BY YAHVAH AND UNSTOPPABLE, UNLESS HE RELENTS.

THE ETERNAL WAVE FLOWS IN AND OUT THREW THESE LIVING WATERS OF ETERNAL LIFE, PERPETUALLY, IN THE RIGHT SEASON OF TIME.

THE FLOWERS OF THE BOWS OF MY LIVING TREES BRING FORTH GOOD FRUIT WITH GOOD SEED EVERY SEASON.

THEY ARE POLLINATED BY YAHSHUA'S BEES THE LIVING WORD OF YAH.

THE HONEY FROM THESE BOWS IS THE RESTORED WORD OF YAHVAH.

I HAVE NO NEED TO WANT OR FEAR

HIS RIVERS OF ETERNAL LIVING WATERS WILL SUSTAIN ME IN THE MIDST OF ALL MY NEEDS AND MAKE ME FLOURISH AND THRIVE.

HIS BODY AND BLOOD FLOW THREW THE ETERNAL LIVING WATERS AND HAVE MADE ME NOT GUILTY IN THE NAME OF YAHSHUA THE CHRIST.

HIS BODY AND BLOOD FLOW THREW MY ROOTS AND MAKE ME WHOLE AND DISEASE FREE.

MY ROOTS FLOW DEEPLY INTO THESE LIVING WATERS AND PRODUCE NEW GOOD FRUIT DAILY WITH GOOD SEEDS.

THESE LIVING WATERS OF LIFE FLOW INTO MY VEINS AND SUSTAIN ME ETERNALLY.

THE WATERS ARE DISEASE FREE, PURE AND HOLY AND THEY SUSTAIN ME DAILY.

I CAME FROM HIS SEEDS THAT HE RAISED.

HE PLANTED ME FIRMLY ON SOLID FERTILIZED SOIL, NOW MY FRUITS FALL INTO THE RIVER OF LIFE, FROM MY BOWS, AND FLOW ONTO GOOD FERTILE SOIL ON THE BANKS OF HIS HOLY RIVER OF LIFE. NEW SAPLINGS COME FROM MY HOLY SEEDS AND THEY WILL PRODUCE FRUIT IN THERE OWN SEASONS.

I AM NOW A GREAT TREE WITH LIVING ROOTS GROWING AND FLOWING ON THE BANKS OF THE LIVING RAINBOW RIVER OF LIFE, THE ONLY ETERNAL LIVING WATERS.

I AM NOW ONE OF THE RAINBOW RIVERS LIVING ORCHARDS.

NOW MY LIMBS AND LEAVES SHADE THE RIVER TO KEEP IT TEMPERATE AND PEST FREE.

THE POWER OF THE LIVING RAINBOW RIVER NOW FLOWS FROM MY HANDS AND BODY. THIS FLOW WILL CAUSE TOTAL INCORRUPTIBLE HEALING OF YOUR BODY AND MIND.

I AM NOT A GRAFT ON TO AN OLD PERISHING ROOT SYSTEM.

I CAME FROM GOOD SEEDS PRODUCED BY YAHVAH. MY ROOTS ARE FROM GOOD STOCK AND THEY ARE CONNECTED TO THIS NEVER ENDING RIVER OF LIFE.

I AM AN INDIVIDUAL TREE AMONG MANY HE PLANTED FIRMLY ON THE BANKS OF THE ETERNAL LIVING RIVER OF LIFE.

I AM AN INDEPENDENT LIVING TREE, BUT I WORK IN UNITY WITH ALL LIVING THINGS.

I WEAR A CROWN THAT HE HAS GIVEN ME FREELY, BUT I HAVE LAID IT AT HIS FEET FOR HE SUSTAINS ME NOT THE CROWN.

SO I AM SUBJECT TO HIM FOR REDEEMING ME OF ALL MY SINS BECAUSE ONLY HE ENDURED THE UNENDURABLE FOR ME, AND I CAN'T OUT LOVE HIM.

AND SO, THEN I AM SUBJECT TO MY INNER GUIDE THE HOLY SPIRIT OF YAHVAH.

AND SO, THEN ULTIMATELY AND INTIMATELY, I AM SUBJECT TO YAHVAH LORD OF ALL, FOREVER FOR EVERYTHING! SO NOW LIVING TREES THAT ALWAYS PRODUCE GOOD FRUIT IN THE RIGHT SEASON ARE NOW SURROUNDING ME ALWAYS.

JWG 5/16/12

I AM A PRIEST
I AM A PRIEST
I AM A PRIEST

1 AM A PRIEST AFTER ADAM, NOAH, ABRAM, MELCHISADEK, MOSES, SAMUEL, ELIJAH, ELISHA, YOHANAH AND YAHSHUA, WHICH WERE ALL PRIESTS OF A DIFFERENT ORDER THAN THE FALSE RELIGION YOU PRACTICE AND FOLLOW.

THEY LOVED ONE ANOTHER AS THEMSELVES.

THEY DID NOT PRACI'ICE JUDAISM, BUDDHISM, CHRISTIANITY, ISLAM OR ANY OTHER FALSE RELIGION OR ISM. THEY ALL DID NOT EXIST AT THAT TIME, SECULAR AND RELIGIOUS MEN CREATED RELIGION TO CONTROL MANKIND AND KEEP THEM FROM THEIR TRUE DESTINY IN LIFE, TO KEEP THEM IN THE SAME PLACE A SLAVE TO MEN BY RELIGION.

THEY WERE REAL MEN THAT WALKED BY GRACE AND FAITH IN THE SPIRIT NOT BY THE LETTER OF THE LAW.

THEY WORSHIPED YAHVAH IN RESPECT AND TRUTH. THEY DID NOT HAVE A FAULT FINDING SPIRIT!

AS A PRIEST OF THIS ORDER, I, MUST WORSHIP HIM EVERYDAY OF MY LIFE WITH MY WHOLE HEART, MIND, SPIRIT AND SOUL.

I MUST REPENT DAILY.

HE CHOSE ME TO BE A PRIEST OF THIS ORDER AND IT ALONE.

NO OTHER YAH'S OR RELIGIONS DO I FOLLOW.

I AM A PRIEST OF THIS ORDER AND NO OTHER GODS DO I FOLLOW.

I WORSHIP HIM AND HIM ALONE.

HE AND I, AND I AND HIM, ARE NOW ONE IN UNITY AND SPIRIT, YOKED TOGETHER BECAUSE WE NOW WALK BY THE SPIRIT OF TRUTH.

AS I DO THIS, THE PAST GETS LOST IN OBSCURITY, THE FUTURE BECOMES THE PRESENT, THE UNFINISHED TRANSLATES INTO THE FINISHED, AND THE UNDONE BECOMES DONE.

I WILL ONLY WALK WITH HIM ALONE FOREVER. HALLELUYAHVAHSHUA!

WALKING WITH YAHSHUA. THE ONLY CHRIST MESSIAH, IS A RELATIONSHIP WITH THE HOLY TRINITY, NOT A RELIGION.
7/5/16

APPENDIX

A COMPARISON OF APES AND MAN

The resemblances and differences between man and the closest of his living relatives, the four great apes, are shown in the drawings and table below. The sketches of the body have been drawn to scale, and have been depicted here with all hair removed for unobscured comparison of the contours of the head and body.

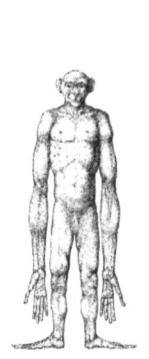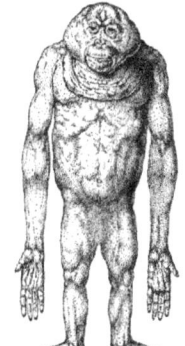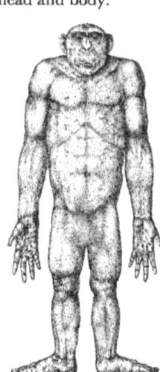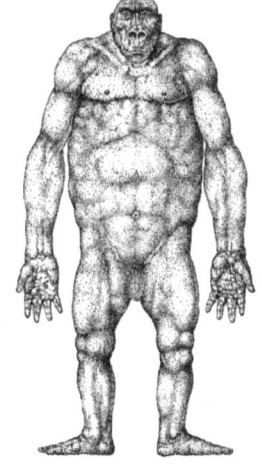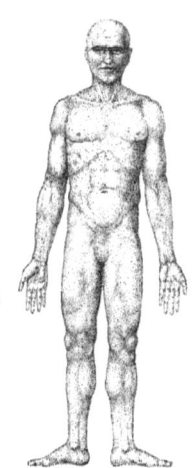

	GIBBON *Hylobatidae*	**ORANGUTAN** *Pongo pygmaeus*	**CHIMPANZEE** *Pan trolodytes*	**GORILLA** *Gorilla gorilla*	**MAN** *Homo sapiens*
NUMBER OF SPIECES	4 species 15 subspecies	1 species 2 subspecies	1 species	1 species 2 subspecies	1 species
AVERAGE HEIGHT	2.3 feet	4.8 ft (male) 3.0 ft (female)	5.0 ft (male) 4.3 ft (female)	6.0 ft (male) 4.3 ft (female)	5.6-5.8 ft (male) 4.11 to 5.3 ft (female)

AVERAGE WEIGHT					
11 to 21 lbs	110 to 165 lbs	125 to 150 lbs	150 to 450 lbs		146 to 158 lbs (male) 107 to 126 lbs (female)
SOCIAL UNIT					
Small Family units of 2 to 6	Small family bands. Least gregarious; males may live alone	Family bands of about 6; often join other bands. Very gregarious	Family bands. Less gregarious than chimpanzees		Families, clans, tribe, sovereign states
DIET AND FOOD HABITS					
Mostly leaves, grass, and fruits; also insects, snails, frogs, young birds' eggs	Predominantly fruit eaters; some leaves and bark	Essentially vegetarian; fruit, leaves, shoots, buds	Completely vegetarian; young leaves, berries, bark, roots, grains, fruits		Omnivores
CRANIAL CAPACITY					
5.95 to 7.60 cu. In	23.5 to 30.0 cu. In	23.1 to 27.0 cu. In	27.9 to 38.3 cu. In		61 to 113 cu. In
AGE AT SEXUAL MATURITY					
5 to 8 years	10 to 12 years	7 to 12 years	7 to 10 years		10 to 17 years
GESTATION PERIOD					
200 to 212 days	233 days	202 to 261 days (231 average)	268 days		280 days (American)
AVERAGE LONGEVITY					
30 years*	30 years*	35 years*	25 to 30 years		69.4 years (American)
ESTIMATED POPULATION					
200,000+	5,000-	100,000	15,000-		8,400,000,000

*Based on animals in captivity

ABOUT THE AUTHOR

James Garner is a prophet, masters, doctor, archeologist, general contractor, plumber, electrician, roofer, teacher, and founder of His Way Ministries. As a child, he spent time in the library as much as possible and even made his parents leave him in libraries in larger towns. Then he graduated high school at seventeen, joined the navy at seventeen, and left navy at twenty. He worked in shipyards for four years. He started contracting and have done so for thirty years. He wrote this book under the guidance of Yahshua and his angels. It is meant to get you to accept Jesus the Christ as Messiah and to restore his holy name to the word and to remove the law from the word.

Printed by Libri Plureos GmbH in Hamburg, Germany